ASIA'S
TRANSFORMATION

The **ISEAS – Yusof Ishak Institute** (formerly Institute of Southeast Asian Studies) is an autonomous organization established in 1968. It is a regional centre dedicated to the study of socio-political, security, and economic trends and developments in Southeast Asia and its wider geostrategic and economic environment. The Institute's research programmes are grouped under Regional Economic Studies (RES), Regional Strategic and Political Studies (RSPS), and Regional Social and Cultural Studies (RSCS). The Institute is also home to the ASEAN Studies Centre (ASC), the Singapore APEC Study Centre, and the Temasek History Research Centre (THRC).

ISEAS Publishing, an established academic press, has issued more than 2,000 books and journals. It is the largest scholarly publisher of research about Southeast Asia from within the region. ISEAS Publishing works with many other academic and trade publishers and distributors to disseminate important research and analyses from and about Southeast Asia to the rest of the world.

ASIA'S
TRANSFORMATION
FROM ECONOMIC GLOBALIZATION TO REGIONALIZATION

JOERGEN OERSTROEM MOELLER

YUSOF ISHAK INSTITUTE

First published in Singapore in 2021 by
ISEAS Publishing
30 Heng Mui Keng Terrace
Singapore 119614

Email: publish@iseas.edu.sg
Website: bookshop.iseas.edu.sg

All rights reserved. No part of this publication may be reproduced, stored in a retrieval system, or transmitted in any form or by any means, electronic, mechanical, photocopying, recording or otherwise, without the prior permission of the ISEAS – Yusof Ishak Institute.

© 2021 ISEAS – Yusof Ishak Institute, Singapore

The responsibility for facts and opinions in this publication rests exclusively with the author and his interpretations do not necessarily reflect the views or the policy of the publisher or its supporters.

ISEAS Library Cataloguing-in-Publication Data

Names: Møller, J. Ørstrøm.
Title: Asia's transformation : from economic globalization to regionalization / by Joergen Oerstroem Moeller.
Description: Singapore : ISEAS – Yusof Ishak Institute, 2021. | Includes bibliographical references.
Identifiers: ISBN 9789814881227 (paperback) | 9789814881234 (PDF) | 9789814881241 (epub)
Subjects: LCSH: Asia—Economic conditions—21st century. | Asia—Politics and government—21st century. | Asia—Civilization. | Asia—Forecasting.
Classification: LCC HC412 M72

Typeset by Stallion Press (S) Pte Ltd

Contents

Preface vii

1. Introduction: Is Civilization Heading Towards a Collapse? 1
2. The Cocktail of Capitalism, Technology and Globalization Turns Toxic 17
3. Democracy 35
4. The Nation-State 65
5. Significance of the Global Financial Crisis 95
6. Global Economics Horizon 2035 105
7. Globalization to Regionalization 117
8. The Power Game in Asia 137
9. Conclusions 155

Epilogue: COVID-19 161
Index 181
About the Author 195

Preface

Since my last book, *The Veil of Circumstance: Technology, Values, Dehumanization and the Future of Economics and Politics*, published in 2016, the world has undergone dramatic changes. Digitalization has undermined and replaced well-known structures, forcing nation-states to develop new technology, to figure out how to use it, and to analyse the interactions with the established parameters of power. The power game is increasingly about gaining the technological edge.

The winner may not necessarily be the nation-state in possession of the "best" technology. The interaction between technology and human beings may be more important than the technology itself. How to mobilize and maximize the skills of people with the technology and how technology is used to rally people around a common purpose will be the crux. This is becoming increasingly difficult because of the diverse social networks and the diffusion of power.

The cocktail of "capitalism, technology and globalization" worked wonderfully for decades, but the number of social losers and disenfranchised people has grown, sowing discontent and frustration. A gap has opened up between the elite and the discontented. The global financial crisis disclosed the fragility of the existing economic model and political system. The negative side effects of globalization are becoming increasingly evident.

Statistics for economics, trade and investment show a tendency for stronger regionalization. The drive for the technological edge has pushed superpowers to look for partners in the region, with the result that countries in the region have been pushed towards a stronger link with the regional superpower. These superpowers have scaled down their commitments to the global system, as they are unable to offer the same level of "protection" as they had in previous decades.

In Asia this is visible in China's drive for its Belt and Road Initiative (BRI), and even more so in its tremendous efforts to be a global technological leader in such areas as artificial intelligence and 5G, and perhaps also biotechnology. As globalization fades, it will be difficult to thrive outside an economic space—impacting on technology, communication, energy, and possibly currency—defined by China. India, Japan and Southeast Asia may not be large enough to contest this development, but they are strong enough to prevent China from becoming too dominant—the dependency is not one way, as China needs them almost as much as they need China.

The outlook until around about 2035 will be framed by relatively well-known elements. Beyond that time frame, the reaction of people to the fundamental question of what kind of relationship human beings want with one another in an age of digitalization and biotechnology may produce a world picture completely different from the one we see today.

The adage "it is difficult to predict, especially about the future" is credited to my Danish compatriot Niels Bohr, who was awarded the 1922 Nobel Prize in Physics "for his services in the investigation of the structure of atoms and of the radiation emanating from them". There is however no proof that he was the first to discover this principle, but he may well have been the first scientist to use it.

This book presents proof that it is indeed difficult to make predictions. It tries nonetheless to do so through a mixture of analysis and projections. Working with our knowledge of how the world currently is can take us some of the way towards meaningful predictions. However, it is rare for the curve for the comings decades to follow the trajectory of the past decade. Indeed, seeking to predict beyond five to ten years, or even shorter intervals nowadays, compels the author to move into uncharted waters. The challenge is to guess at what point the curve will break. I have tried to make these projections by combining guesswork with emerging trends, relying on interdisciplinary and sectoral models, and by using history as a guide. The result is bound to be a personal view. Other observers might draw different conclusions from the scant and uncertain knowledge available.

Many friends in Denmark and from around the world have helped me. But, writing after more than twenty-two years spent in Singapore, I have mainly profited enormously from my Singaporean friends who have been willingly to make themselves available to listen to and participate in brainstorming and discussions. Many ideas and points of view have passed across the table. My friends have shown indulgence, even if sometimes we went over the same ground again and again. Any flaws, mistakes, wrong interpretations or hazardous predictions are my own fault.

I am grateful to the ISEAS – Yusof Ishak Institute for housing me from 2018 to 2020 to conduct research and to write this book. Let me also thank ISEAS Publishing for their excellent help in publishing it.

My wife, Thanh Kieu Moeller, has supported me with all her love, without which the book would not have been written.

Joergen Oerstroem Moeller

1

Introduction: Is Civilization Heading Towards a Collapse?

Civilization is a complex, fragile and vulnerable structure that ultimately depends on people's willingness to act in conformity with certain unwritten rules. This does not always filter through to the governing elite, the businesses and the people, all of whom take the cohesiveness of societies and responses to challenges for granted. Analyses of past civilizations disclose that civilizations succumbed to complacency, external changes such as climate factors, and internal strife, mainly about who governed and distributed the wealth.

Unfortunately, our civilization shows signs of all three of these elements. Complacency is widespread. The political leadership target short-term results, neglecting the long-term negative repercussions. This is combined with a worrying tendency among populations to take what has been achieved for granted. The unattractive fact that the outgoing generation has had to strive to get where they are has been put aside and replaced by a feeling that this is our right. External changes such as climate change and resource scarcities are well-known. But, despite a number of declarations and lip service, they fail to be transformed into policies. Internally, a growing gap between those who are rich and powerful and those who are not threatens to break up societies, mainly because the rich and powerful refuse to share what they have, alienating the majority of people who feel they have no chance of upward social mobility.

The past three to four generations plus the one currently in charge crafted a social contract—how to shape and maintain social cohesiveness among people living in the same society. This entailed a reasonable degree of caring for others combined with empathy and understanding of inclusive growth. That kept us going for quite a long time.

The impact of human beings on nature, however, was neglected, with pollution and the loss of diversity being the consequences. It is possible that the twentieth century—should we manage to avoid wiping out our civilization—will be classified as the greatest robbery, in the sense that we plundered nature, disregarding other species and future generations. Perhaps a kinder label might be the century of egoism/selfishness.

***

Domestically, most industrialized countries moved towards some kind of welfare society, establishing policies to help people in need and introducing an often-complex system of taxation, reflecting progressive taxes to finance welfare. It was most obvious in Northern Europe, but not exclusive to that part of the world. President Eisenhower's expansion of social security in the 1950s reflected the same basic attitude. It bears little if any resemblance to what is seen today. President Roosevelt's new deal introduced in the 1930s and the British Beveridge Report from 1942 constituted a break with the past and steered societies towards cohesion and inclusive growth.

Internationally, decolonization, combined with the United Nations system, anchored in the rule of law. Institutions empowered to enforce a growing international world order sent the same message. The world moved—slowly, admittedly—towards global governance and a sense of sharing of wealth. Both domestically and internationally, various kinds of discrimination were rolled back, albeit they were still visible under the surface. These roses were not without their thorns, but the underlying trend was clear enough.

Over the last thirty years, this trend has given way to an egoistic behavioural pattern. And not only are the political systems unable to control these tremendous changes, but it looks increasingly like the dysfunctionality of models, systems and policies designed during the industrial age will become the norm. Such changes are often described and analysed in a technological and economic framework displaying a technocratic point of view. This is to look at the problem through the wrong end of the microscope. Basically, it is about human nature. Or, to be more precise, it is about people's ability and willingness to adjust, adapt and tune into opportunities and problems brought to them by new technologies. The fundamental factor is how new technology interferes with interaction among human beings, bringing about a new behavioural pattern—a new ethics and moral yardstick.

Apparently we have learned very little from nature. When something new takes place in the natural world, ecosystems begin to adapt and adjust by themselves. This is not done by a prescript or command structure, but by inbuilt mechanisms in the ecosystem, which do not need to be told what to do.

***

1. Information and Communication Technology (ICT)

People love to communicate. Three major changes have influenced relations among human beings since the advent of the internet. First, initiating communication is no longer the privilege of the elite via newspapers, the radio or television; nowadays the large majority can do so via social networks. Second, communication has become global, doing away with the nation-state's monopoly of informing its citizens. Third, the speed of communication combined with the cascade effect gives overwhelming power to those able to catch the attention of other people. To this should be added that anybody can communicate with anybody else, anytime, anywhere about anything.

The door is open to a colossal amount of information, forcing an individual into a screen-out process, changing mindsets and strengthening bonds among like-minded people at the cost of implicitly and perhaps unintentionally skipping inconvenient information. In reality the consequence has been a narrowing mindset, crowding out tolerance and respect for other human beings and their views.

2. Biotechnology

For the first time in its existence, humanity possess the ability to tinker with life, making it now appropriate to ask two simple questions. The first is do we fully understand and appreciate what the long-term effects of such tinkering might be? Perhaps nature is like an iceberg, with only ten per cent showing above the water and the rest hidden beyond the capacity of the human brain. It is rather wishful thinking that nature will willingly surrender all its secret to mankind. The second question is what does it mean to be human when we can change life? Some decades ahead, parents will be able to pick the genetic traits of their child. If they do this, will it then still be their child?

Humanity is also moving towards making death reversible. In 2019 a team from the Yale School of Medicine performed an experiment entailing the partial revival of a pig's brain after decapitation. Pig's brains are not so different in their structure from human brains, so theoretically the same process should be possible with a human brain. The implications of this are mind boggling. Does it mean we can revive people classified as brain dead? And, if so, what does this mean for the limit drawn between life and death?[1]

Possibly the biggest risk to humanity is the combination of genetic engineering and artificial intelligence in the hands of political systems pursuing the elusive but tempting goal of creating a new type of human being defined by political preference. Such an idea was an integral part of Nazism and Fascism, and it is present in communist ideology. It is wishful thinking—again—to expect that when such technologies become available they will not to be used by political ideologies.

As political systems may employ genetic engineering, the business sector may use it for food production. We already see to a frightening degree the narrowing of the types of plants, cereals and animals used to produce our food. This is because the kinds of animals—cows, for example—and cereals have not only been limited to those producing the most meat and milk but they have been genetically modified to deliver more. A potential catastrophic outbreak of a disease could take place as alternative species, those perhaps with a greater diversity of resistances, have been crowded out of the whole process. Will the food we eat in the near future come from "factories" instead of animals and plants?

It is no coincidence that the foundation of nature is diversity. The reason behind this is the logic of the ecosystem—a total system—where species support one another. Our political and economic perspective is fast destroying diversity. An increasing number of animal species are becoming extinct or are getting close to it. Attention has recently been called to how fast the numbers of insects have been falling.[2] According to a United Nations report, one million plants and animal species are on the verge of extinction, eroding "the foundations of our economies, livelihoods, food security, health and quality of life worldwide".[3]

By moving towards a kind of monopolization of the globe and its resources for itself, humanity has been silently—but, strangely enough, knowingly—digging its own grave by destroying the diversity underpinning the ecosystem we depend on. It is an illusion to imagine that human life can continue with the current speed of destruction of other kinds of life.

The situation also reveals the unpleasant ethics that humanity believes we have the right to wipe out many forms of life that have been here much longer than us.

3. Pandemics

An epidemic, also in the shape of a pandemic, is not a new phenomenon. Plagues and epidemics have ravaged mankind for thousands of years. Like climate change, pandemics have frequently explained seminal political and economic change.

Archaeology reveals that the oldest known epidemic took place about five thousand years ago in a prehistoric village in China. Around 430 BC, an epidemic struck Athens at the height of a war with another Greek city state, Sparta. It is estimated that in the region of a hundred thousand people died, undermining the power of Athens and contributing to its defeat. In AD 165–180 the Roman Empire was hit by a plague that claimed about five million lives—historians believe this to be one of the reasons behind the decline of Rome as a great power.

The Black Death ravaged Europe between 1346 and 1356, killing about half of the population. This massive haemorrhage caused far-reaching societal changes, and it may have contributed to the end of serfdom. In the sixteenth century, about ninety per cent of the populations of the Inca and Aztec empires perished when the Spanish conquerors brought along diseases unknown to them.

In the twentieth century, the pandemic known as the Spanish Flu killed around fifty million people worldwide. The main reason for its spread was the exhaustion and malnutrition as a result of World War I. In 1957–58, the Asian Flu caused the death of a million people.

The world has over the past half century become a smaller place in the sense that economic globalization has resulted in millions of people moving around through tourism and migration. The falling cost of air travel has meant they move fast, making it difficult for countries to protect themselves. Furthermore, it is costly for nation-states to erect barriers, as economic globalization makes them dependent on other nation-states. Disrupting the global supply chain is possible for a short time, but without changing the whole economic structure, it is not viable for the long run.

The challenge—already visible in Asia during the SARS epidemic (2002–4)—is to reconcile efforts to fight an epidemic whilst maintaining participation in economic globalization. Most of the nations affected by SARS were able to do this successfully, but one of the reasons for this was the limited number of cases and the fact of the disease being transmissible only when clear symptoms were exhibited—8,096 cases worldwide, resulting in 774 deaths—which made selective measures effective.

In recent decades scientists have discussed the likelihood of pandemics. The conclusion seems to be that the world will need to get used to pandemics in the future, without however giving much by way of specifics as to how often or how serious they will be. This makes it difficult to build adequate defences.

4. Climate Change and Water Shortage

One consequence of this narrow and egoistic behaviour is seen in climate change. The earth is a closed system. Emissions must be absorbed or they will accumulate somewhere. When more comes out of a factory chimney, it changes the existing balance in the global ecosystem, which reacts. Climate change is a counter-attack by nature. There may be others which we have not yet discerned.

Climate change is almost certain to trigger major upheavals as once fertile regions become less so and areas formerly unsuitable for agriculture suddenly become viable. And this is not to forget the studies that predict two billion people will be climate-change refugees by the year 2100 if ocean levels rise at the rate projected.[4] The effect will be mass migration as people are forced to move for the simple reason that they cannot survive where they are. Populations situated in prosperous and fertile regions will defend themselves against the vast influx of foreigners. In short, climate change could be the catalyst for a global conflict for scarce resources, breaking down what might remain of the world order.

An estimated 800 million people live in more than 570 coastal cities vulnerable to a sea-level rise of 0.5 metres by 2050. The majority are in Asia, with China alone accounting for about 80 million of those living in areas slated to be affected.[5] The following cities could end up underwater as sea levels rise: Jakarta, Bangkok, Lagos, Dhaka, Shanghai, London and Houston.[6]

According to the World Resources Institute,[7] water is becoming so scarce in certain areas around the globe that a severe crisis is looming. Seventeen countries, home to almost a quarter of the global population, face extremely high levels of baseline water stress. Another twenty-six face high water stress. The Middle East and North Africa are the most water-stressed regions, but Southern Europe and Turkey, Northeast China, the Southwestern United States and parts of Mexico, and large parts of India will also be affected. Not surprisingly, the effects of climate change and water shortages will combine to make it difficult to cultivate the soil or to perform manufacturing, leading to deteriorating living conditions.

The combination of people being hit globally by climate change, water shortages or both is frightening, auguring billions of people without any prospects of living where they were born.

As is the case for pandemics, climate change has often triggered the rise or fall of great empires. Many historians take the view that climate variability leading to agricultural instability contributed to the decline and fall of the Roman Empire. Rome's economic basis was eroded and the barbarians living at the periphery of the empire saw a decline in their agricultural resources, forcing them to move west and south.

The temple complex of Angkor Wat served as the capital of the Khmer Empire. It is believed that changes in rainfall damaged the sophisticated water supply system that underpinned its economy, and this is one of the main reasons for its collapse.

The Mongol Empire was dependent on livestock to support its economy. Horses were also used for communication, and not the least for warfare. In the first decades of the thirteenth century the climate changed abruptly, with drought replaced by heavy rainfall, resulting in abundant grasslands. This happened simultaneously with the rise to power of Genghis Khan, and it probably contributed to the dynamism of the Mongol Empire under him and his immediate successors.

***

Pandemics and climate change may be some of the main reasons behind the rise and fall of nations and empires. It is also almost certain that in the future mankind will be confronted with further upheavals leading to geopolitical change.

5. Use of Medicine

The human body is genetically engineered to repair itself and to fight disease. Nonetheless, it is no coincidence that people die from disease. Perhaps we are genetically engineered to die at a much younger age than is seen around the world. Maybe nature intends to create its own defence against some of these diseases, but is prevented from doing so by human intervention. Perhaps other diseases form part of the nature-human relationship. Maybe some diseases have a role in the ecosystem that we do not understand.

The fact that we interfere in the system by fighting diseases with medicine—however laudable and perhaps however much people struck by such diseases appreciate it—means that in the long run we weaken our own immune systems. In the very long run, this may lead to total dependence on medicine because a weakened immune system is no longer able to do the job. A possible outcome could be similar to the effect of the loss of natural diversity, with us running the risk that one day nature will strike back with bacteria and diseases that medicine is unable to combat.

Irresponsibility in disposing of unused medicines is widespread, with most people just throwing them in the garbage can. The long-term effect of such behaviour on nature is devastating.

6. Use of Chemicals

Chemicals have found their way into our daily lives in unprecedented ways. Agriculture is heavily dependent on pesticides, insecticides and fertilizers. Most cleaning materials contains chemicals. The list is endless. The conventional wisdom is that the use of chemicals is harmless—at least if used properly—but common sense raises a question mark over the long-term consequence on nature of the steady and increasing outpouring of chemical substances that are not organic and consequently cannot be absorbed by the ecosystem.

Some of this can be classified as a pollution problem, with at least some countries taking action against toxic substances. But equally dangerous may be the long-term consequences of what are regarded as harmless chemicals slowly accumulating in human beings, animals and plants—in short destroying the ecosystem without us noticing it.

***

Biotechnology, medicine and chemicals have one common denominator. They are tools used by mankind to create an artificial world—to eliminate nature's own way of working and to replace it with a way chosen by mankind to serve us from the narrow and short-term perspective of what is profitable defined by economics. One wonders whether such a world is compatible with the survival of the present civilization—or perhaps even of mankind over the longer term.

7. Age of Anthropocene[8]

Until about the year 1900, nature defined the environment for human activity. Human beings had to adjust to nature and to live in conformity with nature and the ecosystem. Since then, mankind has gradually but surely turned the tables. And we now live in an era where humans have a strong impact on the ecosystems, forcing them to adjust, with climate change being an example of this, although not the only one.

But the Age of Anthropocene has already been overtaken by a new age, which has not yet been labelled, allowing the use of the *Age of Irresponsibility*. Human beings can now through biotechnology and artificial intelligence change nature and the ecosystems, creating a non-natural world—a world in which mankind interferes in the holy grail of determining what life is and what it means.

8. Demographics

By the year 2100, the global population—presuming no major wars in the interim—could reach nine to ten billion people. Contrary to the case of the past, a large share of this population will be the elderly, who will need to be supported by the reducing share of people in the working-age bracket. The burden is heavy, and will grow heavier year by year. Even worse, it constitutes a break with nature. Before mankind started to use medicine, the composition would be a large number of young people and a very small number of people above forty years of age—the number of grandparents was small. From a rather brutal perspective, it can be said that humans were here to ensure a new generation was born, and having done so, and after having taken care of their offspring, they would pass away. From the 1500s onward and till around the year 1800, life expectancy throughout Europe hovered between thirty and forty years of age.

It is doubtful whether the earth can continue to deliver the resources with such a large global population increasingly looking for a good life. Add to this the socio-economic problem that a proportion of them (those aged above sixty-five years)—and in some countries this group may account for more than forty per cent—will not contribute to production, but they still ask for a good life. A clash with the working age group of the population is possible, perhaps even likely. It will be a major political problem to find the money and the manpower to cater to the demands of the elderly. Furthermore, the largest share of people will live in areas with lower living standard than the richer parts of the globe, which points to a geopolitical clash between the minority defending their privileged position.

9. Political Elite Decoupling from the Population

Another fracture threatening cohesiveness is that the elite no longer feels responsibility for governing the nation-state. In fact, members of a nation's elite distance themselves from their less-educated fellow nationals and instead communicate with and regard themselves as part of a global elite instead. They may carry the same passport, but they do not have much in common.

The elite travel, live and work with little regard for the nation-state they originated from, contrary to the situation for the less-educated people who feel increasingly left behind with no option to prosper from globalization—their horizon is the nation-state. A good life for them is becoming increasingly difficult to achieve as the elite seize an ever-growing share of wealth while at the same time coming close to monopolizing access to the top schools and universities for their children.

10. Education

The road into higher education opening the door for upward social mobility may be blocked for those without rich parents, even if some schemes exist to help poorer students financially. There are stories in the mass media of how parents have presented ivy league universities with gifts or donations in order to have their children accepted there, even if they have a mediocre academic record.[9]

The paradox is that the masses now have levels of education sufficient to contest decisions by the leadership but not good enough to offer alternatives. The implications are that the masses voice their dissatisfaction with the decisions and failures of the elite, as the example of the global financial crisis illustrated. But if members of the masses get into power, they display a similar failure to govern, very often accentuated by populism and nationalism for the simple reason that a map to navigate this uncharted terrain does not exist.

The schism between the national elite and the masses has been accentuated by the transformation of top universities into intellectual multinational enterprises that attract an increasing share of students from abroad, crowding out national students in the process. For the academic year 2018/19, 30.33 per cent of all students enrolled at Massachusetts Institute of Technology came from abroad.[10]

11. Social Losers

The shift from manufacturing to information and communication (the audio-visual economy) has produced a large number of social losers. The skilled worker in an industrial plant was the king during the manufacturing age. Now such individuals have lost their jobs and possess skills for which there is no longer any use. For the most part they are too old to adapt to new jobs, and the jobs remaining to them are largely lower paid ones in the services sector, which they reject. Over the decades they have insisted that politicians bring their old jobs back and reintroduce industries such as steel plants and car factories. The political opposition have promised to do this, but as soon as they get into power they adopt policies analogous to those of the previous governments. The skilled workers feel betrayed and they are unable to accept that technologies such as robotics and outsourcing cannot be rolled back.

They have reacted by voting not for the opposition but against the system. This explains Donald Trump's victory, Brexit and the coming into power of the Five Star Movement and Lega Nord in Italy. These individuals became social losers and reached the conclusion they had nothing further to lose by voting against the system because they had already lost everything they had.

The result is that the countries that once represented the core of manufacturing strength now harbour a class of disgruntled people who are deeply dissatisfied with the system and who feel they have been abandoned by the elite that are synonymous with the system. Judged by history, such feelings constitute a fundamental threat to the system, and the situation is becoming worse as the system has apparently given up, with the elite being unable or unwilling to share with the social losers.

12. Falling Belief in the System—Pessimism about the Future

People can sense that something is wrong. The feeling that the system does not work for "me" is one that is especially strong among social losers. According to the 2019 Edelman Trust Barometer,[11] trust in the future is found in only 6 of the 26 nation-states analysed,[12] with 6 expressing neutral responses and 14 indicating distrust. Digging a little deeper, the analysis discloses three fundamental gaps threatening the cohesion of nation-states and the global system.

The first fundamental gap is that trust is almost exclusively found in emerging markets or developing economies (EMDE), with China at the top followed by Indonesia, India, the United Arab Emirates and Singapore. Of the 14 nation-states expressing distrust, 11 are industrialized, with the United Kingdom, Ireland, Spain, Japan and Russia at the bottom. The only industrialized country in the bracket expressing a neutral response is the Netherlands. This bodes ill for a concerted international effort to tackle the global problems that will be decisive for the future of the current civilization.

The second one is the trust inequality showing a gap equalling the previous highest point between the informed public and the mass population at 16 percentage points. Asked whether they believe they and their families would be better off in five years' time, these two gaps are confirmed, with not a single industrialized country among the top ten and not a single EMDE among the bottom ten. With one exception (Russia), the informed public took a more positive view on the future than the mass population.

The third one is whether the system works for "me", with 20 per cent of the mass population and 21 per cent of the informed public saying *yes*. Figures of 72 per cent of the mass population and 74 per cent of the informed public felt the situation was one of injustice. And 24 per cent of the mass population and 17 per cent of the informed public expressed a lack of hope.

Key Points

These findings make it pertinent to analyse how the political systems and economic model function, to be followed by an attempt to sketch out what will take place over the next fifteen years. How will the system react under the seminal changes casting their shadow over the future of mankind? How have these changes influenced the mindsets of political leaders and business leaders? Can we find any trace of these fundamental changes in the behaviour of nation-states in defining priorities for their security policies?

In the following chapters, we will look at seven elements that determine how the system works, and what the implications of this are for the future.

1. The interaction among capitalism, technology and globalization
2. Democracy
3. The nation-state and multinational companies
4. What the global financial crisis meant for the global system
5. How the world will look in a horizon 2035 analysis
6. The rise of regionalization replacing globalization
7. The future of Asia in this context

It will become clear that mankind is no way near to addressing the twelve fundamental changes, and it continues to steer a course set by ideas and norms surviving from the last decades of the twentieth century. The guiding principle is still the market economy emphasizing short-term profit for private enterprises and without incorporating social effects, degradation of the environment or exploitation of non-renewable resources.

The two main threads of the analysis and conclusion put forward in this book are the move from globalization to regionalization and the role of social networks dividing instead of unifying people.

The global superpower, the United States, no longer possesses sufficient economic, technological and military power to set a course for the globe—even less the future of civilization. Nor does its population want to pay the price of being an icon. China, seen as the most likely successor, cannot succeed because of demographics, dependence on outside countries to feed its population, overdependence on imported energy, and the lack of a developed service industry with a worldwide reach. Unlike the case with the United States in its glory days, China is not likely to be seen as a model for other countries. Hence, we move towards a regional world.

The paradox of social media is that technically—the infrastructure is there—they push the globe towards globalization, but people use the global networks and the opportunities provided to exchange views worldwide to deepen disagreements and denigrate the views of others. A kind of intellectual and conceptual fragmentation takes over. The role of social networks has given rise to a power struggle between the states and the big data companies. This has been exacerbated by increasing concerns about privacy, cybercrime and the abuse of the net, often seen in the context of fake news. This leaves a good many people uncertain about which information is true, leading them to look in vain for guidance and hence falling easy prey to imposters.

Notes

1. Christof Koch, "Is Death Reversible", *Scientific American*, October 2019, pp. 26–29.
2. https://www.nationalgeographic.com/animals/2019/02/why-insect-populations-are-plummeting-and-why-it-matters/.
3. https://www.washingtonpost.com/climate-environment/2019/05/06/one-million-species-face-extinction-un-panel-says-humans-will-suffer-result/?utm_term=.0582987ec3c9.
4. https://www.sciencedaily.com/releases/2017/06/170626105746.htm.
5. World Economic Forum, *The Global Risk Report 2019*, http://www3.weforum.org/docs/WEF_Global_Risks_Report_2019.pdf.
6. https://www.ecowatch.com/cities-vulnerable-sea-level-rise-2610208792.html.
7. https://www.wri.org/blog/2019/08/17-countries-home-one-quarter-world-population-face-extremely-high-water-stress.
8. The Age of Anthropocene is defined as significant human impact on the earth's geology and ecosystem.
9. https://www.theguardian.com/commentisfree/2018/oct/21/what-will-help-you-get-into-harvard-super-rich-parents.
10. https://iso.mit.edu/general-statistics-2018-2019.
11. https://www.edelman.com/sites/g/files/aatuss191/files/2019-02/2019_Edelman_Trust_Barometer_Global_Report.pdf.
12. The Trust Index is the average percentage trust in NGOs, businesses, governments and media.

2

The Cocktail of Capitalism, Technology and Globalization Turns Toxic

Until the turn of the century, behavioural patterns controlling political systems and the economic model were fairly predictable. Political leaders and economic decision makers not only followed an analogous script but their actions were transparent and other players knew the game and the rules—including the unwritten ones—so surprises were few.

The new thing is that the game has become unpredictable. This is the case for globalization and domestic policies, making it hard to navigate them.

In the past, nation-states complied with the decisions and rulings of international institutions such as the Security Council of the United Nations, the International Monetary Fund, the World Bank and the World Trade Organization because they expected other nation-states to do the same. This is also the case with the question often asked as to why member states of the European Union (EU) comply with the rulings of the European Court of Justice when it is powerless to enforce its rulings.

The global system was in reality not global. It was a global projection of the salient elements of the American political system and economic model. The rest of the world acquiesced because the American model had proved its worth. It actually worked and worked well. The United States was the guardian of the system, ready to step in if needed to make sure it worked. The rule of law underpinning the system was American, and perhaps British, law. Economically, the United States and Britain in the early 1950s commanded close to half of global gross domestic product (GDP). Other nation-states had to acquiesce, as the alternative was that they would not get access to the markets of these two countries. From around 1991—when the Soviet empire collapsed—until the first decade of the twenty-first century, these two countries in reality took it upon themselves to force other countries to toe the line and to accept the existing global order. The two Iraq wars and the sanctions against Myanmar serve as examples of the posture of the United States and Britain as self-proclaimed defenders of globalization, which even justified military intervention against countries that did not respect the rules of the game. There was some expectation that Russia under Boris Yeltsin would join the global order, and some observers expected China also to move in the same direction.

It looked as if the United States would have been able craft a global order in its image provided it had been willing to share some of its power and to allow a stronger role for international institutions. However, the Clinton administration eschewed this window of opportunity and moved towards using American power to pursue American interests. Such a policy became a cornerstone of the Bush administration, with the United States depicted as a superpower, or even a hyperpower, either acting alone or leading a coalition of the willing in demolishing the chances that might have existed for transforming the global order.

The Trump administration has made it clear that the United States does not see the established global order as the foundation of its foreign policy or of its security policy. It actually wants to act alone and it has adopted a policy of "America first", which transitions into a policy of "America only". Britain—the other founding father of the post-World War II system—coined the slogan "take back control" during the Brexit debate in 2016.

Both countries have abandoned their role as pillars of the global system, which consequently is starting to crack. Domestic policies have changed in almost all industrialized countries under the weight of social networks, social and economic inequalities and migration.

A new kind of political leader has surfaced. Many of them borrow political slogans and policies from populism, nationalism and xenophobia. They are unwilling, and possibly incapable, of reading the mindset of their political opponents, and they feel vindicated in their own narrow-minded policies. The mutual respect that formerly existed among political leaders has gone.

President Trump is an example of this new type of politician. It is not the case that he has no rules. He has. And it is not that he does not know what he wants to do. But his rules are different from those we see as the established rules–rules which still form the basis of the actions of his political opponents. A similar case can be seen while watching political leaders such as President Erdogan of Turkey, President Putin of Russia and the political leaders in Poland and Hungary. They have thrown away the unwritten rules that underpinned political power play in their countries, catching their opponents and the establishment wrong-footed. Notions of fair play and respectable behaviour are not in their rule book. It is bizarre to watch how they get away with changing positions on core issues without any kind of explaining, outmanoeuvring their opponents and the establishment, who do not know what to do when confronted with such behaviour.

What used to be a predictable power game that followed a known rule book has been transformed into a situation of unpredictability. These new leaders have succeeded at this because they are better able to communicate with the population and they do not care about their relations with the establishment. They read the mindsets of a large share of the people better than the traditional politicians who talk and act like part of the establishment—those who have lost credibility since the global financial crisis of 2008–9. These new leaders do not feel the need to explain their policies. Rather, they speak in short, hard-hitting sentences that appeal to ordinary people, who as a result feel they are finally being taken seriously by a politician who speaks a language they can understand.

The explanation for this paradigm shift can be found in analysing how the interactions among capitalism, technology and globalization have changed.

Since the end of World War II, the dominant economic model by far has been capitalism. It has overshadowed both the centrally planned alternative offered by the Soviet Union and the import substitution policies tried by a number of developing countries.

Technology, broadly speaking, had not changed much until the 1970s, but since then has brought about a revolution in daily life not seen since the start of the industrial age of the late decades of the eighteenth century.

Globalization gradually placed its mark on economic activities. Up until the 1970s this was still not as significant as is was just prior to the beginning of World War I in 1914.[1] As was the case with technology, globalization changed dramatically during the two decades of the 1970s and the 1980s. According to the World Bank, trade as a percentage of GDP was 17 per cent in 1970, rising to 71 per cent in 2017.[2]

The remarkable thing has been how well these three parameters have interacted with one another in delivering growth to a majority of countries, combined with an increasing living standard. More and more countries rallied around this model. In 1991, the challenger—the Soviet Union—collapsed, which in the eyes of many countries confirmed the effectiveness of capitalism, technology and globalization.

The hope that such a model could receive global approval proved to be short-lived. First the Asian financial crisis of 1997–98 sowed doubt, followed by the global financial crisis of 2008–9, and this doubt has since grown in strength. The model has ceased to function in a balanced way, and its negative side-effects—what could be called external diseconomies—are becoming stronger.

Capitalism

Pollution and the Ecosphere

The cost of pollution in many countries has become so high that it eats up a considerable share of GDP. Several studies, including one from the World Bank about the situation in China, point to a total cost amounting to about a third of growth. On 4 March 2014, Chinese premier Li Keqiang told an audience of almost three thousand delegates at the National People's Congress, and with many more watching live on state television, "We will resolutely declare war against pollution as we declared war against poverty." This is a war that, according to newspaper reports, China is winning.[3]

The fight against pollution, however laudable, is rather narrow and is aimed at what may broadly speaking be called direct pollution from production—industrial, services and agriculture. Goals such as a hundred per cent recycling are rarely integrated in economic models. The same goes for such guidelines as how much pollution is seen, and how large a use of resources is used to produce a new item of goods with a lower emission of carbon dioxide (the product cycle). It is, for example, far from certain that a new fridge producing lower emissions would be better for the environment than simply using an old one and not bringing a new product cycle into the calculation. The same goes for the life cycles of products and the importance of looking at how much pollution a new product generates over its life, particularly at the time to replace an existing product. Many electronic devices such as cell phones have a much longer technical life than a commercial life, meaning that they are replaced with new models even while they are still perfectly functional.

It is regrettable that very little is being done to prevent pollution in the first place, which is a result of the manufacturing process.

Even less is being done to transform societies and economic thinking in tackling the use of chemicals and medicines. The economic model still reflects short-term profits for the business sector, producing rising share prices in the interests of management and owners.[4] No genuine attempt has been made nationally or internationally to shift the horizon and introduce a new value system of upgrading the ecosphere and long-term conditions for the interactions between human beings and nature. Economic transactions are still dictated by what is best for economic growth. This is understandable, as a large proportion of the global population lives in relative poverty and has a palpable need for improvement. But the rich countries that could and should have taken the lead in starting such a transformative process have not done so.

Calculations have been made about the effect on the global economy of global warming.[5] Almost all of these calculations either look at isolated events such as floods attributed to climate change or at how much nation-states spend on curbing emissions. These are superficial analyses. The real cost is what it will cost mankind if the rise in sea levels makes large areas uninhabitable for human beings. In Asia, for example in large areas of Bangladesh, Jakarta, Bangkok and many other cities, people have been forced to leave and to live elsewhere.

What is required is a series of economic analyses that will seek to put a price on maintaining the ecosphere as it is. To this should be added the cost of pumping chemicals and other manmade substances into the natural world, deteriorating its quality.

Capitalism Has Proved Itself a Wonderful Growth Machine

From 1820, when industrialization first took off, until 2014, global GDP rose from US$1.2 trillion to US$104 trillion, an increase of almost a hundredfold. The increase from 1950 (at US$9.25 trillion) to the same end point saw about a tenfold increase. From 1981, when information and communication technology started to have an impact on the economy, up until today, global GDP has increased about threefold.[6] Since 1945, millions of people in developing countries have been lifted from poverty. The growth trend has continued over the last twenty-five years despite setbacks such as the Asian financial crisis in 1997–8 and the global financial crisis in 2008–9.

This is magnificent. The problem is that the negative side-effects—always present, as is the case for example with pollution—over the last twenty-five years have grown to dominate the social, political and economic picture of capitalism. The question is quite simply whether the majority would be better off not benefitting from this growth and whether the quality of life would be better with lower growth.

The negative side-effect (external diseconomy) attracting the highest attention is the issue of the rising *inequality of income and wealth*. Figures from the United States illustrate how income and wealth increasingly go to a minority of people, leaving the rest with an income more or less the same. A study from 2014 reveals that in the late 1930s both the top 0.1 per cent and the 90 per cent at the bottom owned around 20 per cent of total wealth, with the middle class (roughly speaking) accounting for 60 per cent. In 1985 the share of the top 0.1 per cent had fallen to 10 per cent, with the share of the bottom 90 per cent increasing to 36 per cent. The middle class had 54 per cent. Inequality had declined. But then it started to rise, and quickly. In 2014 the top 0.1 per cent increased their share to 17 per cent, and the bottom 90 per cent saw a decline to the same figure (17 per cent). Or, in other words, over the last thirty years the already rich saw an increase of

70 per cent and the share for the bottom 90 per cent has been cut by half.[7] By any measure, this is a colossal rise in inequality.[8] Bloomberg & Credit Suisse suggest that the planet's 138 richest people currently command more wealth than the roughly 3.5 billion who make up the poorest half of the global population.[9]

Multinational companies use the free market model and globalization to harvest large profits. This underpins a *concentration of business activities*, as these multinationals buy smaller companies around the globe. A total of 1,318 companies control 80 per cent of global business activities. Of these, 147 account for 40 per cent.[10] The share of total sales by large firms rose between the years 2000 and 2014. In the United States, the top eight companies increased their share from 28 per cent to 37 per cent, and the top four saw an increase from 22 per cent to 28 per cent. In the European Union, the corresponding figures are from 35 per cent to 37 per cent and from 25 per cent to 26 per cent.[11] The Big Six US banks—JP Morgan, Bank of America, Citigroup, Wells Fargo, Goldman Sachs, and Morgan Stanley—in 1995 had assets worth 17 per cent of US GDP. Less than twenty years later their combined assets reached 60 per cent of GDP.[12] The treasure chest owned by the big companies is enormous. Some years ago, the value of this chest was estimated at US$1.73 trillion, of which technological companies accounted for US$690 billion, with Apple alone representing US$178 billion.[13] These funds are used to buy companies on the rise, either to incorporate their technology into the plans of the large companies or to eliminate them as future competitors. Oracle serves as an example of this, having used more than US$40 billion to buy other companies.[14] Such a large concentration opens avenues for abuses of power and distorts the workings of the economy. It can also hardly be said to be in conformity with competitive markets. In reality, it pulls the economy towards an extractive model, where the big companies arrogate to themselves a large share of economic growth.

The industrial age was, until the later part of the twentieth century, characterized by plants and factories, steelworks, mines, abattoirs or other contributors to manufacturing *spread out over a country*. Many towns had a plant serving as its backbone offering jobs to several thousand workers; the spin off was jobs in other sectors of the economy such as the services industry, banking and retail. In a way it represented a self-sustaining economy for the town.

This picture has been completely obliterated. Driving through towns in most industrial countries, empty factory buildings catch the eye. Production has been moved to larger units concentrated in cities, or to emerging markets and developing economies, or has disappeared because of new technology. Towns have become deserted as people can no longer find jobs there and have moved to the cities. What was formerly the periphery has gradually turned into a kind of wasteland. Fifty years ago, my own country, Denmark, with a population of five million, had seven shipyards outside the capital city of Copenhagen. About half of them served as the foundation of the economic life of a town with a population of 25,000. Now these shipyards are all gone.

Economically these changes may be profitable. But this process of uprooting many people and of leaving the mainly elderly behind in towns without any economic activity and only scaled-back or even dismantled public services produces geographical inequality on top of the rising economic inequality. The idea of a nation in balance, where the living standard did not differ much regardless of the areas where people lived, belongs to history.

The labour share of GDP has fallen significantly over the last fifty years in major industrialized countries. Up until 1975, the labour share in the United States hovered around half of GDP, but it has since fallen to a little over 40 per cent. This fall has mainly taken place since 2001.[15] OECD statistics reveal that between 1970 and 2014 the labour share has fallen between 6 per cent and 13 per cent for the following G20 countries, in order of magnitude: Italy, Korea, the United States, Japan, Australia, Canada, Germany, France and the United Kingdom.[16]

There may be several explanations for this phenomenon. One of them might be that new technology is more expensive and, in some cases, riskier to develop, which requires a higher remuneration for capital than labour. Another is that new technology encroaches on manpower, requiring fewer workers, with the inevitable result of a lower share of revenue going to labour remuneration, both because of fewer workers and as a result of greater competition for jobs—wages are suppressed by market forces.

The social and political consequence is that labour feels that capitalism is not a fair economic model. It reduces the number of jobs in traditional sectors, provides a smaller remuneration for work, and the labour market is split by the combination of outsourcing, offshoring and new technology such as robotics. One part of the employment market is asking for highly skilled people, while another is offering low-paid jobs in the services sector. The victims of this dichotomization are the skilled workers in the industrial economy.

The ManpowerGroup worked out that from 2006 to 2011 between 30 and 40 per cent of employers found it difficult to fill positions and were forced to keep them vacant because people with the right skills were not available. In 2018, 45 per cent of employers around the world indicated that they struggled to fill roles, with skilled trades workers, sales representatives and engineers the most difficult to find.[17] At the same time, people possessing a degree—but a "wrong" one, that did not equip them with the skills that were in demand—had to work in jobs they were overqualified for, for lower wages than they expected. A total of 14 out of 18 European countries saw a rise in the graduated workforce for jobs that do not really need graduate skills. For 11 of these countries, the share of jobs in this category was above 40 per cent.[18]

Capitalism had not only increased income and wealth inequality but it has *divided the labour market*, making a large number of people social losers and thereby undermining political stability. Increasingly, capitalism is dividing nation-states according to skills and education.

Statistics from the United States disclose the extent of these social and political problems by analysing by ethnicity the number of jobs added or lost between 2007 and 2015. About 8 million jobs were added. Hispanics, Blacks and Asians gained close to 9 million jobs, while Whites lost about a million.[19] The analysis does not provide any explanation, but knowing that the number of manufacturing jobs declined by 1.4 million in the same period (and by 5 million between the years 2000 and 2015),[20] there can be little doubt that White people lost jobs in manufacturing while the three other ethnic groups took jobs in the services sector, where most of the jobs were created.

The social implication is that skilled workers lost their jobs and were offered lower paid jobs that did not require their skills, but they did not want to take up these offers. They became social losers. Perhaps by choice, because they might have continued to be employed but they preferred to stay unemployed in the hope that their jobs might come back. These people were doing very well in the heyday of manufacturing. In fact, they were the pillar of the manufacturing society, determining by their numbers and influence who would be in power. Now they have suddenly found themselves close to the bottom of the social strata. A change that many of them could not cope with. They turned against the system, feeling that they had been sacrificed and that they had not been listened to.

It may be hazardous, but there are many indications to show that capitalism is the economic model that still delivers the highest economic growth. At the same time, however, it distorts the economy and has spin-off effects on social and political stability. Too many people are left feeling that they do not get their fair share of the increased wealth. They shift this dissatisfaction to politics, creating a cleavage between the elite (possessing a degree or similar) and the rest of the population, in particular those without a degree.

There has been a flow of reports, analyses and studies, in addition to policy measures, advocating that the labour force should receive training to enhance their skills. Whilst this is not wrong, possibly the biggest challenge will be the need to provide jobs for the say 10 to 15 per cent of the labour force that cannot acquire such skills. Simply speaking, there is a segment of the population that is suited only to simple manual jobs. As most of these functions have either been taken over by robotics or information technology (for example, security in car parks) or have been axed to save costs, these individuals are left without employment. The economic model has made it profitable to remove these jobs because the societal costs are not integrated into the model—the costs have instead been shifted from businesses to society, making it free for businesses to transfer the burden to society as a whole.

Technology

Technology refers to the tools used by humans. All too often it is overlooked that the effects of new technology on society are dependent on humans using such technology. Analysing why technology belongs to the cocktail turning toxic is therefore a question of how good humans are in using new technology and the degree to which new technology disrupts relationships between humans and tools and among human beings.[21]

New technology in the industrial age—such as washing machines, automobiles and dishwashers—took more than the span of one generation to reach a saturation point of eighty per cent of American households. The telephone was invented in 1876, but it had to wait more than a hundred years to reach the same level of penetration.

For new technology in the information age such as the internet, social media and cellular phones, the penetration time to reach eighty per cent of households was between ten and twenty years—in fact it was closer to ten than to twenty years.

Both waves of technology disrupted the ways in which society operates—the relationship between citizens and public authorities, business activities, the family structure and human relations. A citizen could not continue to look after their interests without mastering the new technology. The difference between the two though is that the first wave offered time to adjust to, to adapt and to absorb the new technology. The second wave behaves more like a tsunami, confronting citizens with the need to adjust to, adapt and absorb within a decade or two. It is a colossal disruption.

As was seen when analysing capitalism, it leaves a large number of people with an education and a degree that are close to useless. Businesses find it difficult to find workers with the skills that are in demand. The education system is under pressure to change so that graduates will have the skills that will be in demand in the future, but because of the speed of the transformation it is in the dark about what these skills will be.

Figures for research and development (R&D) by the major players in the game about the technological edge are well known. The United States tops the list (latest data available in US$ billions) with 511, followed by China at 452, Japan 165, Germany 118, South Korea 92, India 66, France 63, the United Kingdom 60, Brazil 45, and Russia 42.[22] There is no real surprise to these figures. They reveal that the United States is still at the top and that the gap with China is narrowing.

What the figures do not disclose is how these countries are preparing their populations to apply the new technologies. How good are their universities in spotting future trends? How good is the government in rolling out online services in a form that people will be able to understand? How much retraining and courses to learn new skills are available.

Based on anecdotal evidence, it seems that the United States should not be at the top of such a list. China has fast been introducing new technologies and it looks like the Chinese population is ready and perhaps even eager to absorb it. Nowadays it is difficult to pay for anything in China with cash, as almost every economic transaction takes place over platforms offered by the major Chinese companies, and the cellular phone has replaced the wallet.

It is also difficult to find analyses about how much effort major countries have devoted to what may be called technology assessments. That is, studies to examine the societal effects—both positive and negative—of the technologies before they are introduced. In other words, how much effort is being put into changing behavioural patterns to cope with the introduction of new technologies. And in the case of external diseconomies, what is being done to address them.[23]

The winner in the game of future technology may not necessarily be the one pouring the most money into R&D, but could instead be the nation-state most able to maintain coherence and avoid disruption. Applied in a clumsy way, many examples of new technology could lead to societal dislocation that threatens to tear society apart, or could at the least produce a large and growing class of people that feel left behind.

It is difficult to estimate, but a rough guess would point to a figure of around ten per cent of the population who cannot or will not adapt to use new technology and who cannot fill job functions other than those entailing manual work. To not solve this problem would be a millstone around the neck. Economically it would be a huge waste of manpower. In social terms it would not be something that a country would be proud of, and the people in such a position will be the social losers. Politically, they would then turn against society.

Globalization

The world is divided over whether economic globalization is good or bad. A large number of emerging markets and developing countries see globalization as a force for good in the world. In countries such as Vietnam, the Philippines and India, more than eighty per cent of their populations are of the opinion that it is a force for good. At the bottom of the scale we find Britain, the United State and France, with less than fifty per cent of their populations expressing this sentiment.[24] The explanation for this is not difficult to find. For almost all EMDEs, globalization has brought about a significant rise in GDP per capita and lifted millions of people out of poverty.

Even more important than economics is the political and psychological effect of moving from the status of a developing nation caught in a poverty trap to having economic growth at a much higher level than the industrialized countries. People in these countries, simply speaking, see themselves as being catapulted into another league, now being taken seriously, and often out-competing their former colonial masters. They have found a voice in international negotiations. They feel they have arrived by sheer willpower and hard work.

The other side of the coin is the former "rich" countries that now have a lacklustre growth rate of around 2 per cent—sometimes a little higher, sometimes a little lower—but dismal compared to those of the EMDEs. Jobs have moved to the EMDEs, primarily to Asia, with the effect that manufacturing has transited to Asia. For all OECD countries, manufacturing value added as a share of GDP had fallen from 17.7 per cent in the early 1990s to 14.3 per cent by 2016. For the United States the corresponding figures are 16 per cent and 11.6 per cent; for Britain, 16.6 per cent and 9.2 per cent. One industrialized country maintaining a strong manufacturing sector is Germany, but even here there has been a decline from 24.9 per cent to 20.7 per cent. Japan has done better than the other G7 countries, with a figure that moved from 23.5 per cent down to only to 21 per cent. The reason for Japan retaining its manufacturing strength to a large degree has been its proximity to the Asian growth centres and its ability to play an important role in China's manufacturing.[25]

The developed countries see themselves as losers in the global game, especially recalling that for decades after the end of World War II they were the winners, exporting manufacturing goods and importing raw materials and benefitting from favourable terms of trade.

This poses problems for the global system. It was designed by the two strongest powers—the United States and Britain—when they accounted for close to half of global GDP. Even if it was labelled as being global, the idea was to forge a system benefitting these two countries. They were willing to accept the costs and commitments necessary to make the system work, which by far were outweighed by the benefits. It was profitable for them.

The shift in the global economy broadly speaking starting in 1979 with Deng Xiaoping's reforms, which meant that gradually the system began to benefit other countries—EMDEs and especially China. The foundation of the system was the free market economy anchored in competition and the free movement of capital—foreign investments. The United States and Britain (at least in the early days) had economic structures that benefitted from such a model. Former competitors like Germany and Japan were out of the game, with their countries in ruins. The Soviet Union was exhausted by its war efforts. The developing world was confined to primary products. The United States and Britain were the only countries in the world with a manufacturing sector worthy of that name. Now the tables have turned, with China and several other Asian countries as big exporters, and with the global savings surplus having moving from the United States to countries in Asia and the Middle East.

The newly benefiting countries look at the system and use it to their advantage. Because competitiveness has shifted in their favour, they reap the benefits, whilst at the same time their contribution to running the system is not very high. This means they reap large net benefits compared to the United States and Britain, who are beginning to be net losers, or to at least see themselves as such.

The reaction from the United States has been to seek to prevent other countries from using the system to their benefit. This can be seen in its withdrawal from the Trans-Pacific Partnership, in its renegotiating of the North American Free Trade Agreement, in its talk of a trade war with China, and in its efforts to undermine the World Trade Organization. It is almost as if the United States is taking the stance that it was happy to benefit from the system whilst it was in its favour, but now that the situation has changed, then the system must also be changed. If that cannot be done, then it will make changes unilaterally.

Not surprisingly, the rest of the world, including the EU, which finds itself in a similar economic position to that of the United States, regards such a policy as exhibiting double standards. The result is, however, that the strongest global power has adopted a policy of dismantling the global system, replacing it with unilateralism—which for the United States means America first, or even America only—while no other nation-state or grouping such as the EU is sufficiently strong to take over as leader. Yes, they are strong enough to prevent a complete dismantling and to maintain the basic structures at least for now. They are not strong enough, however, to be able to broaden and expand the system in order to bring it into the new era with a more balanced global economy and new technology, asking for rules about trade in services and transfers of technology.

Key Points

The cornerstone of the economic model of the twentieth century—a hundred years that witnessed unprecedented economic growth—has failed over the first two decades of the twenty-first century. The model was acclaimed as delivering high economic growth. And whilst it still does this, the global trend of this growth has been falling. The main argument for adopting this model is therefore weakening, giving rise to criticism that spills over into attacks on the model. It has lost its primogeniture status.

Marks against the model include income and wealth inequality in particular and the sense among an increasing share of the population that it is unfair in that it maintains privileges for the rich and restricts upwards social mobility. The number of social losers is increasing, causing them to revolt against the model. The inability of the model to achieve its crowning achievement—high economic growth—combined with the negative side effects, has seen the movement against it spill over into and undermining the accompanying political system of liberal representative democracy. These interactions between a faltering economic model and an impotent political system open the door for a major crisis for what used to be the leading economic and political powers in the world: the Western democracies.

Notes

1. Globalization prior to World War I was however only for a select group of rich, industrialized countries, with the rest of the world either supplying resources or agricultural goods or not in the game. Compared to the share of the global population involved in globalization, the pre-1914 model shows only a low figure.
2. https://data.worldbank.org/indicator/ne.trd.gnfs.zs.

3. https://www.nytimes.com/2018/03/12/upshot/china-pollution-environment-longer-lives.html.
4. I have dealt with this, pointing out the flaws of economics and offering some prescriptions about how to transform the model, in my earlier volume, *The Veil of Circumstance: Technology, Values, Dehumanization and the Future of Economics and Politics* (Singapore: ISEAS — Yusof Ishak Institute, 2016).
5. See, for example, https://unfccc.int/news/the-cost-of-climate-change.
6. Fixed prices (US$2011). https://ourworldindata.org/grapher/world-gdp-over-the-last-two-millennia?time=1..2015.
7. http://gabriel-zucman.eu/files/SaezZucman2014.pdf.
8. Saez and Zucman, *QJE 2016*. DB Global Market Research.
9. http://www.bloomberg.com/news/2014-02-04/is-inequality-approaching-a-tipping-point-.html.
10. http://www.welt.de/wirtschaft/article13680359/Diese-Firmen-bestimmen-Schicksal-der-Weltwirtschaft.html.
11. *The Economist*, 17 November 2018.
12. *The Economist*, 16 May 2015.
13. Ibid.
14. http://www.bloomberg.com/news/2011-12-20/oracle-misses-estimates-as-clients-throttle-tech-spending-shares-decline.html.
15. https://www.nytimes.com/2013/01/13/sunday-review/americas-productivity-climbs-but-wages-stagnate.html?_r=0.
16. https://www.oecd.org/g20/topics/employment-and-social-policy/The-Labour-Share-in-G20-Economies.pdf.
17. https://www.manpowergroup.com/media-center/news-releases/Talent+Shortages+at+Record+High+45+of+Employers+Around+the+World+Report+Difficulty+Filling+Roles.
18. European Social Survey, *The Conversation*.
19. Economic Cycle Research Institute.
20. https://www.epi.org/publication/manufacturing-job-loss-trade-not-productivity-is-the-culprit/.
21. These observations go back to 1971 when I heard a lecture by Emmanuel G. Mesthene, then director of Harvard University's Program on Technology and Society. http://www.americanphilosophy.com/techne/mesthene.html.
22. https://en.wikipedia.org/wiki/List_of_countries_by_research_and_development_spending.
23. The first attempt to do so may have been an initiative by US Congressman Daddario in 1967 to introduce a bill to "provide a method for identifying, assessing, publicizing, and dealing with the implications and effects of

applied research and technology". https://www.ncbi.nlm.nih.gov/pmc/articles/PMC4270161/#fn61.
24. Deutsche Bank research, March 2018.
25. The figures from all the countries mentioned do not start at the same date, which explain why the starting year is not given as more precisely than the early 1990s. https://data.worldbank.org/indicator/nv.ind.manf.zs.

3

Democracy[1]

Spinoza's Prediction

The Jewish-Dutch philosopher Spinoza (1632–77) predicted that democracy would be guided by and taken over by demagogues jettisoning reason and logic. Freedom for individuals in whatever way it was seen when Spinoza lived would be there, but the mediocrity of rulers would lead to chaos. The elite would rebel against such a system. The people would be confronted with the choice between freedom and chaos versus order and tyranny. Spinoza predicted that people would choose order and tyranny. Men are by nature unequal, and equality among unequals is an absurdity. Therefore, a system which Spinoza labels aristocracy or monarchy, with the ablest individuals in charge, would inevitably prevail.

It is thought provoking that the BBC in February 2017[2] published a localized breakdown of voting patterns determining the outcome of the British referendum to leave the European Union of 23 June 2016 (the Brexit referendum). The report says that "a statistical analysis of the data obtained for over a thousand individual local government wards confirms how the strength of the local Leave vote was strongly associated with lower educational qualifications. Wards where the population had fewer qualifications tended to have a higher Leave vote.... If the proportion of the local electorate with a degree or similar qualification was one percentage point lower, then on average the leave vote was higher by nearly one percentage point." History will tell whether the decision to leave was good or bad for Britain, but, as the data reveals, it was decided by the less educated, while the higher educated would have liked Britain to stay. Moreover, those earning most of the money to keep Britain going, including welfare payments, are found among the higher educated.

Six Major Problems

How Representative is Democracy?

Liberal, representative democracy is supposed to produce a parliament and government congruent with the electorate. It does not always turn out this way. Members of parliaments must toe the line to solidify the party's role in blocking legislation across party lines. Sometimes this makes it impossible for the government to find a majority, it overrides the national interest, or prevents members from voting according to their conscience. In the US Congress, members may be regarded as outcasts if they break party discipline. Only John McCain's seniority and status saved him from that fate when in September 2017 he voted against the bill to repeal the Affordable Care Act. In the British Parliament there is a large majority for staying in the EU, but toeing the party line makes it impossible for this large majority to enforce its policies. Instead, Brexit is largely dictated by a small wing of the Conservative Party and ten members of the Northern Ireland DUP. Without their support, Prime Minister May would have been forced to resign earlier or the government would have fallen. Not surprisingly, voters are baffled and in many cases feel cheated. They often find themselves asking the simple question, what has this to do with democracy?

Those Supported by the System versus Those Generating Wealth

In many countries, the number of those supported by the lavish welfare system is creeping close to the number of people working and thereby earning the money to fund welfare payments. The conditions for generating wealth stop being defined by those actually doing it. They are taken over by those not generating the wealth but being supported by the wealth generated by others.

Members of the non-active part of the population do not see welfare payments as something for them to fall back on when they are not able to earn a living because of a recession or other factors complicating their participation in the workforce. They expect and demand that the state offer them opportunities for them to accept or reject; and if they reject such an opening they still expect to claim welfare payments.

Welfare recipients will never be a majority of the electorate, but combined with the staff in local communities and agencies administering welfare, they can come close. Strangely, these two groups form a tacit alliance to defend the system that is directly or indirectly supporting them. For the United States, with two political parties, the possibility to constitute a majority is remote, but not for the many European countries with five or ten political parties. In such a scenario, their votes may be necessary to form a government. Furthermore, when this happens, they demand a continuation of or even an increase in the share of gross domestic product (GDP) allocated to welfare.

The Amount of Welfare Benefits is Growing

Politicians have had to swallow the hard lesson that it is tremendously difficult to scale back welfare provisions once they have been given. Even more pertinent is the fact that elections are won by offering more and higher welfare payments. Political parties have gone into elections trying to appease, to sway and to court the approval of voters.

The change in attitude among voters explains such political platforms. The welfare system worked well initially because voters understood that it was designed to help them in case they were not able to take care of themselves. Many voters had lived in an era where welfare did not exist, and they held back on using it. They accepted the implicit assumption that it was a safety net, and not a substitute for earning a living.

That changed, however, when new cohorts joined the electorate. They had not lived in a society without welfare. They regarded it as something they had the right to tap into. Their parents started by needing support, and they looked for the rules and regulations to support them, and in many cases were both grateful and modest. The next generation started by scrutinizing what they could squeeze out of the system, without linking it to their needs. Many of them looked at welfare payments as a kind of salary, seeing their "job" as being a beneficiary of the system. Costs rose dramatically.

Psychologically, the way the welfare society has developed runs counter to the basic human instinct vital for the self-respect of an individual. That instinct is the feeling that somebody needs you, the satisfaction of contributing to something together with others, and—perhaps most importunately—that society and your fellow citizens demand something from you. A too generous and too automatic welfare system runs the risk that beneficiaries will be put under tutelage by society and transformed into a condition of simply floating along without contributing. This is what happened to the Roman Empire when the once proud people of Rome were transformed into a mob. It may also be what Friedrich Hayek meant when he chose the title of his 1944 book *The Road to Serfdom*.

Politics has Become a Profession

The virtue of liberal, representative democracy was that it was "representative". Broadly speaking, the composition of parliament mirrored the economic segments of society, albeit gender equality was far distant in most countries. Furthermore, most members of parliament had worked for quite a while outside political organizations before they entered parliament, and many of them kept up such work even while serving as MPs. They knew about daily life and had for some time been a citizen like everybody else, meeting fellow citizens in the workplace, while out shopping or among the parents of school children.

The large majority of members elected to parliament by socialist (labour) parties had actually been workers, and a large part of the members elected by parties representing farmers had been or were still farmers. Moreover, they worked their way up, not inside the party machine but within local organizations—for members of socialist parties as spokesmen of local trade unions and for farmers through local associations. In these capacities they negotiated with local organizations (employers or buyers of agricultural goods), and after being elected they would meet those who elected them to defend their decisions face to face. Should they be forced to accept poor terms, they would see the pain or anger in the faces of their fellow workers or farmers. In my own country, Denmark, out of four prime ministers in the 1950s, one was a farmer who ran his farm while prime minister, two were former trade union members who had worked their way up through the ranks, and one was an academic. In Britain, the last prime minister to have such credentials was James Callaghan (1976–79), who started out as a clerk for the Inland Revenue, where he joined the Association of the Officers of Taxes, a trade union. After ten years he quit the civil service to devote himself fully to trade union work. Ronald Reagan was in the 1950s president of the Screen Actors Guild—a labour union with more than a hundred thousand members in the film and television industry.

It is rare to find such people nowadays. Most members of parliaments have been associated with politics from their youth and have worked their way up inside the party machine without much contact with outside life. The risk is that we will end up with a self-centred and self-sustaining political elite that treat politics as a game, deepening the power distance and nourishing the feeling that the system is neither listening to nor caring for the electorate.

Social Networking

This new form of communicating has deprived the political system of its right of initiative; the ability to set the agenda and the near monopoly of communication with the electorate via newspapers, radio and television. Communication is no longer one-way with politicians telling the electorate what they intend to do. It has turned into an interactive phenomenon.

Political parties have been pushed from the status of having a proactive role to being a reactive player running after and trying to respond to questions raised by others. Such a role does not instil confidence among the electorate.

A deeply worrying development has been what has taken place in the United States since the election of Donald Trump, with the president using social networks to spread news and information in a disruptive way. He has apparently bypassed the established system in order to build his own channels with the electorate. He may win in the short term, but the victim of such behaviour will be the system itself, with it having been undermined from the top.

The widespread use of tweeting—with its limit, currently, of 280 characters—introduces an oversimplification of complex issues. The game is about who can win the attention of the most people, and this rules out deeper analyses of the long-term effects of policies.

Fake News

Fake news has become a catchword dominating news and commentaries. In reality it is more complicated than normally perceived, and the phenomenon must be seen in conjunction with the way the human brain works.

Fake news can be divided into disinformation, misinformation and malinformation.[3]

Disinformation is so-called news and observations that are deliberately uploaded to the internet in order to cause harm by purveyors who know very well that the information is fake. The individuals doing this may be motivated by a wish to make money, to gain political influence, or to cause trouble just for the fun of it. The circulation of fake news on the net normally begins with disinformation. This kind of fake news is more easily detected than the next category.

Misinformation is content that is intentionally false but which is spread mainly on the net by persons not knowing it is fake. Those who do so may be motivated by many reasons, but rarely to make money or to gain influence. They may find the information interesting or want to boost their ego. This fake news and those who spread it are more dangerous than disinformation because they do not realize what they are doing, that they are being used by those creating disinformation, and what the deeper implication of their actions can be. Furthermore, there are many such people on the internet who like to do this. They are very active on the net and will often be known by a large number of those receiving their posts, lowering the suspicion that the information is fake

Malinformation is an attempt to twist public opinion during an election. It is the kind of fake news or fake comments that have attracted the greatest attention because this is what was seen during the 2016 presidential election in the United States with Russia allegedly trying to influence the outcome. There have also been analyses about malinformation in Britain's Brexit vote of 26 June 2016.

The most effective and, for social networks, the most dangerous method of disseminating fake news is to start with something that has a kernel of truth to it. Or, best of all, to find an example from everyday life that people can recognize and will relate to. Gradually, the starting point, which is true or at least has elements of truth to it, is twisted so that the comments become malinformation conveying a message that is fundamentally untrue and without readers being aware of the initiators attempt to hoodwink them.[4] Another well-known and equally dangerous tactic is to ensure that the same piece of malinformation, although in a slightly different form, appears from various sources. Those who spread misinformation swallow the bait because they come to trust it after seeing that it comes from multiple sources.

The functioning of the brain explains why fake news in various disguises is successful. A prevailing theory of how the brain works is called predictive coding or predictive processing. The brain attempts to figure out what the input it receives from our senses actually is. It does this by trying to guess what the most likely interpretation is. The way the brain goes about this is by combining prior expectations or experiences—what is stored in the brain—and comparing this with the incoming data. This process determines what the brain classifies as the most reliable interpretation. In the case of fake news, the more an individual can link the information with something he or she has experienced previously, the more likely it will be that the brain will conclude that it is the truth.[5]

Politicians Are Out of Tune with the People, Especially over Immigration

For most people, globalization was all right as long as it meant free trade and foreign investment. But that attitude changed when they met globalization on a personal level and encountered people who behaved differently on account of their different culture, ethnicity or religion. It unsettled them. Not only did globalization threaten their jobs, but their daily lives were also disrupted when the people in the shopping centres, at their workplaces, in their neighbourhoods and at their children's schools turned out to not be like them.

The cultural confrontation is most visible in European countries that are not used to receiving large numbers of migrants. It is especially the case when the new citizens have different behavioural patterns to those who have lived in the country for generations. The following figures show the share of total population not born in the country in which they live: Sweden 18.5 per cent, Austria 15.2 per cent, Germany 14.9 per cent, Norway 13.8 per cent, the United Kingdom 13.2 per cent, France 11.1 per cent, Spain 9.2 per cent, Denmark 9 per cent and Italy 8.3 per cent.[6] If immigrants had been distributed about a country, such figures may still have created a political problem but perhaps one that would have been more manageable. But this is not the case. Reports tell of small towns receiving a large number of refugees who are being lodged in sports halls, turning daily life for people living there upside down.

Immigration is a sensitive issue—one that mixes demography, economics, normative behaviour and ethics. It is becoming an issue now because of globalization and social networks. Globalization has opened the door for people to move across borders on a large scale to find jobs outside their own country. Social networks have made it possible for them to live in a host country while maintaining cultural and societal links to their country of origin. This has become a barrier for integration into their new country, leading to enclaves and "ghettos" for migrants who have no genuine wish to adopt the cultural norms of the country they live in.

The political system has clearly failed to prepare their citizens for an influx of this size. Many of them have over a lifetime paid taxes or been enrolled in government schemes to fund their needs—their health and welfare—after retirement. Now they are confronted with waiting lists for such things as, for example, an operation for a hip replacement. The quality of welfare services has allegedly been deteriorating as staff are being cut. People are told that the government does not have the money for such things, but at the same time they know that money is being spent on migrants. Just how much money depends on the definition of what constitutes a migrant. Looking at the figures for 2015, with the large influx of refugees into Europe, Sweden spent 1.35 per cent and Germany 0.5 per cent of GDP.[7] Citizens feel that this is unfair. They have contributed to taxes in the expectation they would receive benefits, which are not forthcoming to the extent promised and expected. The political system has also neglected to inform immigrants that in choosing to come to a new country the implication is that they should learn how to adjust to the country's norms, and that they cannot expect, and even less demand, that the host country adjusts to them. Immigrants and refugees form enclaves, leading to parallel societies developing. Both citizens and immigrants/refugees feel deluded, with the result that they bear a grudge against each other. The fact that population numbers are falling and that migrants/refugees may be needed in the long run to enter the workforce does not carry much weight.

The problem in the European Union has been aggravated, as there are at least five different groups of migrants, each having their own characteristics and contributing to or burdening a host country's economy differently.

The first group to mention is that facilitated by the free movement of labour inside the EU. This means that a European worker entering, for example, Denmark, irrespective of the member state the individual is from, is eligible to Danish welfare. This situation has given rise to a suspicion of welfare tourism, pointing at citizens from one member state entering another pretending to seek work but actually trying to get fired in order to reap social welfare benefits.

The second group is that of workers from Central and Eastern European countries, which joined the EU in batches in 2004 and 2007. Since then, millions of workers from these countries have migrated to work in Northern European economies such as Germany and Britain. Numerous analyses show that migrant workers from other EU member states pay more in taxes than they receive in benefits, and indeed more than the average citizens of their host nations. In short, it is a good business for the host country.[8] But despite this these migrant workers do not feel welcome, as the slogan "Polish plumber" demonstrated during the Brexit campaign.

The third group of workers is made up of those from neighbouring countries that have an association agreement, such as Turkey, thus opening the door. It is estimated that there are about 2.77 million people of Turkish origin in Germany, close to a million in France and half a million in Britain.[9]

The fourth group is made up of people from former colonies, particularly those of Britain and France, who emigrated after the colonies gained their independence, perhaps because they feared for their security in view of having collaborated with their former colonial masters, or perhaps after having seen the possibility for a better life.

The fifth group is composed of refugees from adjacent countries such as the Balkans, the Middle East and North Africa, plus some countries south of the Sahara.

The view of the average citizen on migrants rarely distinguishes between these five groups. There is an alarming tendency to bundle members of these different groups together under the label "foreigners", and often no effort is made to hide that they are not welcome.

How Privatization Disenfranchises the Poor and Endangers Democracies

Privatization of Public Services Divides the Nation

Public services used to serve a double purpose. The first was to facilitate such things as the provision of electricity, water, transportation and postal services. These services could in principle be offered by the private sector, but that option was rejected in favour of providing a uniform quality of services nationwide. Public services aimed to establish that all citizens were equal, connoting that national solidarity ranked higher than a business model. Keeping the nation together legitimized the fact that citizens in large cities would pay more than the cost price for services, and that by so doing they would be subsidizing the periphery. On average the inhabitants of the large cities would be more affluent than their fellow citizens, so this amounted to progressive taxation.

During the 1980s, the argument that private companies could offer services at a lower price gained traction. This could, however, only be achieved if the market and prices were segmented. Citizens would pay according to the cost of delivering services to where they lived. Such a business model was akin to favouring the big cities to the detriment of the periphery, where the lower population density and a lack of infrastructure made providing the same level of services more expensive. The priorities were reversed. A business model overruled national solidarity, and regressive taxation took over.

Lower prices and higher efficiency were delivered by cutting—sometimes drastically—the services offered to the periphery. Railway lines were closed. The frequency of postal services was reduced. Many services such as libraries, high schools and local hospitals were closed. Citizens were told that much better facilities could be found in the nearby larger towns, which were not so nearby after all. Many citizens moved out of local communities because of this message. Towns practically degenerated into deserts, many of which were home to a dwindling population of elderly people, stoking claims that public services should be cut further in view of the small number of people living there.

As income inequality started to rise in the 1980s, the gulf between the people using private companies and the people using older-model public companies deepened. The quality of public services fell because the most qualified people were lured to work in private companies. A person needing a hip replacement operation but not able to pay for it would have to wait several months, while a person able to pay could get such an operation at a private clinic the next day. The children born to less-affluent parents could not gain access to the nation's top universities because recruiters sought students from top-tier schools, which they could not afford to attend. The public schools could not give children the same quality of education as the private schools.

Those who had been left behind felt they had been sacrificed in pursuit of higher cost benefits or cost efficiency—or whatever slogan was being used—necessary to justify privatization. They did not feel as if they were living in the same nation with equal access to public services. Nations became dichotomized. The anatomy of the Brexit vote in Britain, the protests in France against President Emmanuel Macron, and the populists gaining power in Italy can all be traced back to provinces and the periphery voting against the big cities.

Privatization initially received a tailwind because it looked as if it could save taxpayers money. Few people realized that public companies could have done the same job if they had not had to carry the burden of keeping the nation together. It soon turned out that privatization failed to live up to the promises that accompanied it. Profits and efficiency were achieved by cutting investments and maintenance. After the private companies were sold for a higher price, a handsome profit was reaped. Many nations soon found themselves left with a rundown railway network or a telecommunications system that disregarded the periphery and only delivered services in the big cities, and which were in no way better than those the public companies had offered.

Privatization had also sapped the identities of these nations. The core symbol of being a citizen of a nation—and the one to generate a feeling of pride—is the passport. The authorities of a nation-state used to issue passports. In the past, citizens would go to their local police station to apply for one. This solemn procedure no longer exists. Nowadays the job of issuing passports has been privatized and handed to commercial operators. It may not sound like a big deal, but, conceptually, the signing away of this core function of national identity should not be underestimated.

Dehumanization of Public Services

A dehumanizing of public services has taken place simultaneously with the emergence of information and communication technology (ICT). Links between citizens and the authorities used to be person to person, which was a costly venture. Now they all take place online.

From afar it looks fine. Why bother with the cumbersome and time-consuming process of letters and meetings between officials and citizens when it could all be done through the marvellous instruments of ICT. The argument behind the switch was the same as with the case for privatization: it would be better and cheaper. The disadvantage proved to be the same.

Once again, part of the population was cut off. Many elderly people did not have access to ICTs, and some of those who did were unable to master the intricacies of such indispensable ICT security measures as passwords, email verification and two-factor security. Most nations offered assistance to bridge this gap, but it did not stop people from feeling sidelined, and it often made life difficult because such assistance would not be available in the periphery, which is where many of the elderly lived.

The information needed by the public authorities had to be provided correctly, even meticulously. Submissions deemed to be inaccurate were rejected under the claim that this or that was missing or wrong. People—mostly the elderly and the social losers—can stumble upon receiving such a message and would not know what to do. The option of dealing with a human being is frequently not available. In addition, the move to a mode of online communication transferred some administrative costs to the citizens by asking them to spend time on "paperwork" that would previously have been undertaken by a civil servant in the local community.

Any society or nation depends on trust between its citizens and the authorities. Trust governs a society when citizens feel a public officer's decision would have been the same if the roles had been reversed. In fact, most citizens build an image of the state or public authority not from what they have read or heard but from their own personal experience with the authorities. They only believe social networks and media coverage if it is in harmony with what they have experienced. Personal meetings had offered the opportunity to explain their problems and to argue their case. All of this is lost with a system of online transactions. And whilst it is true that such a system may work well for the large part of the citizenry that belong to the mainstream, it is not the case for those outside it—and they are the ones who need help. The result is that privatization contributes to the dichotomization of a nation.

The human factor and person-to-person communication have been thrown away as nations quickly move towards a system that is opaque and obscure. Citizens do not have the faintest clue about who makes decisions on important issues that could be vital for them. If a decision is not in their favour, then surely they can protest, complain and ask for a review of that decision; but they undertake such steps without any idea of who will respond to them and how a new decision will be reached.

One wonders how this will look when artificial intelligence (AI) enters the game and the systems built around AI take over almost all communication between citizens and public authorities.

To this should be added the risk that mistakes can lead to leaks of data held by public authorities. Personal information about health, taxes and other matters might end up on the internet for everybody to see. The drive to cut costs has led many local public organizations to work with outdated data systems for far too long, which has made it possible for hackers to slip in the backdoor.

There is another more serious and sinister risk to privacy. Private companies that have access to sensitive information and data will have access to private details about citizens. How can citizens feel secure when all their data that they have exchanged with public authorities passes through private companies?

George Orwell wrote about this in his novel *1984*.[10] He warned against some kind of dictatorship controlling all private activities. The key phrase in his book was "Big Brother is watching you". This can happen in the future as more public services are going online, but the immediate risk is that personal contact between citizens and public authorities ceases to exist.

Focus on Money

Ministers, parliamentarians and civil servants used to have a lifestyle comparable to the citizens they ruled. In the past, the rulers and the citizens were two sides of the same coin. Nowadays, leading politicians jump from public office to the business sector. They sell their experience and knowledge to the highest bidder. Once they leave their public position, they join the lecture circuit and ask for (and get) high fees with which to enrich themselves. Civil servants follow in their footsteps and sell their experience and insight into public life and how the executive branch works to the business sector. They trade their job as a civil servant for the lavish life of a business executive. Apparently, public life is a platform for gaining insights, which the private sector will subsequently pay for. But that is not what the voters had in mind when they supported a candidate, nor what they expected when paying the salaries of those civil servants.

This trend breaks the unwritten contract between citizens and politicians/civil servants because citizens initially viewed politicians/civil servants as a group of people who would devote themselves to running the nation. One of the most important differences between democracies and non-democracies was precisely the trust that citizens had in the leaders. Citizens were convinced that those leaders acted in the spirit of "bonus pater familias"—in the interest of the nation and its citizens. That attitude constituted a moral barrier against corruption of power and corruption of money.

The business sector follows a similar pattern. The purpose has always been to earn money—profit—but many corporations had a vested interest in the development of the society in which they operated. They were part of the local culture and knew about the conditions endured by those who worked for them. In 1965, more than four-fifths of all stocks in the United States were owned by individuals. Now individuals own about a third of all stocks.[11]

Additionally, the global financial crisis revealed how reckless and selfish the business sector had started to act. It is estimated that business leaders in the United States are paid 373 times more than the average worker.[12] In almost all other countries it is much lower.[13] In Britain that figure is 133. The idea that business is here to deliver goods and services to the people and act as a stakeholder with a strong interest in society is rapidly disappearing.

Citizens increasingly classify politicians and business leaders as "not like us", and they thus take less of an interest in politics. In Britain, membership of the Conservative Party, Labour Party and Liberal Democrats as a proportion of the electorate fell from close to 6 per cent in 1970 to about 1.5 per cent in 2019. The Conservative Party since 1955 has seen its membership fall from close to three million to the current figure of 124,000.[14] With fewer members, it becomes increasingly difficult to fund the party's activities, making grants from the business sector irresistible. But this comes at the price of cutting links with voters, who look with suspicion on how political parties are funded. In the United States, the average price of winning or holding on to a six-year term in the Senate is $10.5 million; the average price of winning a seat in the House of Representatives is $1.7 million.

It may be to stretch the argument—we may not yet be there—but the trend is clear that political influence and elections can be bought instead of earned.

Legal Rights of the Individual

In 2015 the former British defence chief, Field Marshal Bramall, was having breakfast with his wife when the police without warning entered and searched, or perhaps raided, their house as part of an investigation targeting child sex abuse. No explanation was given. Two years later the police apologized after accepting that the search had been unjustified and should never have taken place. Several former ministers, including former prime minister Edward Heath, were also investigated and their names made public. This all took place because of obscure and undisclosed information given to the police. Yet those who were investigated did not have an opportunity to clear their names as they were not informed of the source behind the investigation.

Citizens also plan according to the law. This presupposes at least three things. First, laws must be written so that an ordinary citizen with a reasonable level of education can understand them. Second, laws must be administered in a transparent way and according to their purpose. Third, laws should only be changed when necessary, and when that becomes the case they should not be pulled from under those expecting the current law to continue. In many democracies, none of these conditions are met.

Law texts nowadays are full of hard-to-understand jargon for most people. The texts not only use complicated and technical language but they are open for interpretation. It is difficult to maintain trust in a political system that is not able to reach out to the average citizens and make it clear what the purpose of a law is. More and more citizens have to fall back on lawyers and, in the case of taxation, auditors to make sure they are on the right side of the law. Inserting a layer of specialists between citizens and public authorities means increasing the power distance, as it soon becomes the specialist and not the citizen who communicates with the authorities.

The hitherto sacrosanct distribution of political power between the legislature, the executive and the judiciary is no longer as visible as it once was.

Many laws confer powers to parliamentary committees to scrutinize and ultimately to decide on recommendations submitted by the executive branch. In doing so, parliaments have set up mini replicas of ministries and agencies vying with each other for executive power. The staff working on parliamentary committees need to disagree with government ministries, otherwise parliamentarians would ask "why are you there?"

In the United States, Supreme Court judges are nominated for life. A president may put his stamp—political and moral orientation—on the Supreme Court for decades ahead. It seems odd to read that with this or that nomination the Supreme Court will lean towards conservative or liberal decisions and that with this or that composition one of the members has the swing vote tipping the scale in a liberal or conservative orientation. Was not the Supreme Court supposed to be politically neutral?

Constitutions often give the Supreme Court the power to rule whether a law passed by parliament is in accordance with the constitution. Legally, such a procedure may seem impeccable. Looking at democracy, however, it is difficult to accept that ten, eleven, or twelve judges nominated by governments over ten or twenty years can overrule decisions taken by a parliament elected by the people. It is hard to deny that the US Supreme Court has turned into a political body.

The tendency to change laws is increasing. This has for many years been the case for tax laws, where to a certain degree it is understandable as the economy makes it natural to need to fine-tune taxation. It is, however, a problem for businesses to see the rules, regulations, taxes and depreciation allowances change, often at short notice and without any consideration for the long-term planning necessary in business. To know for certain about these matters, not only how they look now but for some time into the future, is one of the most important things in running a business, and it is vital for public authorities to provide such certainty.

Several European countries continually change laws controlling immigration. Many immigrants look at the law when entering a country to plan for citizenship only to see criteria—especially how long they have stayed and worked in the host country—being changed again and again.

Continually changing laws used by citizens and businesses for planning is not lawmaking with retroactive effect, but it comes close to being so.

Complacency

Complacency is the enemy of responsibility, effectiveness and efficiency. When liberal, representative democracy won the duel with the Soviet system, politicians and civil servants lost the ardour to deliver good governance.

During the Clinton administration, the United States was the undisputed global leader—some observers labelled it a hyperpower. Its economy was flourishing. The political system worked. The rest of the world looked to America as a role model. This was the moment for an American leader to step forward as Harry Truman did when he was president of the United States (1945–53) to forge a post–World War II system instead of going isolationist or resting on his laurels on account of the policies of a long list of his predecessors. It did not happen. The Clinton administration governed wisely and competently in the sense that no mistakes were made—at least not major ones. But no major new foreign-policy initiatives saw the light of day. The opportunity of an offer—magnanimous as President Truman's was—to share power with the rest of world under new global rules was not grasped, and it was probably not on the radar of the administration or the president.

The last chance to do so came with the terrorist attacks of 11 September 2001. The rest of the world did not hesitate to declare solidarity with the United States. All the other major powers faced similar threats—some had actually suffered from terrorist attacks prior to 9/11. The Bush administration should have sensed a historic opportunity was at hand to shape a global coalition through the United Nations that might have gone further than fighting terrorism. It failed to do so. Instead it opted for a coalition of the willing, and slowly but surely it rejected overtures from other major powers. Perhaps such a coalition could not have been achieved, but it is legitimate to criticize that it was not even attempted.

The rest of the world came to look at liberal, representative democracy and, in particular, America as arrogant and unwilling to understand that the interests of other nations did not necessarily need to toe the US line in order for them to be classified as friends cooperating in running the global system. Since the beginning of World War II in 1939, every American president has been opposed to European authoritarian political systems, from Nazism and Fascism to Communism, and this prevailed during the presidency of George H.W. Bush when the Soviet and Russian empire collapsed. During the Trump administration, the United States flirted openly with semi-authoritarian political systems in Russia, Hungary and Turkey. In just a short span of time the United States lost the moral leadership it had built and defended for more than fifty years.

While the Soviet system was challenging liberal, representative democracy, it constituted a barrier against abuse of power by the ruling elite. They knew that if they went too far in abusing their power, the population could start to look for an alternative. The instinct to concentrate power in a few hands and to allow inequality to increase was kept at bay. It is no wonder that since the end of the Soviet Empire in 1991, the trajectory of falling belief in democracy and rising power distance, plus inequality, have followed the same trend.

Why Social Media Endangers a Free Society

Democracy is fighting for its life. The question is, what can be done to save it? A short analysis on this is given below, followed by eleven propositions.

Liberal, representative democracy is mired in a clash between the less-educated majority and those with higher education. Social networks have sharpened this confrontation by offering the majority something they did not have before: access to the media with the possibility of setting the agenda. The outcome will be determined by how well democracies are able to tackle certain major problems connected with social networks.

The first problem is the need to offer citizens protection of their privacy. Democracy is the only system of government with powers invested in the people preventing abuse from the government, by the simple fact that any government can be ejected from power at the next election.

The second problem is the need to get it across to citizens that social networks are theirs and that they need to take ownership of them. It is up to citizens to prevent fake news or similar harmful information; for example, outsiders interfering in elections to obtain the outcome they wish. The US presidential election in 2016 is seen as the best example. John Locke (1632–1704) hit on the right idea by saying that freedom depends on a degree of self-discipline among those who enjoy this privilege. The same approach can prevent social networks from being hijacked by destructive forces and turn them into an instrument supporting—not disrupting—liberal representative democracy. The free access to social networks can only survive if the users—the people—emerge as its guardians and weed out abuse and fake news, stopping those who seek to use it to delude and deceive.

A third problem is the abuse of social networks by terrorists and cybercriminals. Terrorists use the net to maintain communication, thus undermining efforts by the authorities to fight terrorism. A study reveals that the cybercrime economy has resulted in US$1.5 trillion in illicit profits being acquired, laundered, spent and reinvested. This figure is higher than Australia's GDP. A breakdown of this amount reveals the following: US$860 billion of illicit/illegal online markets, US$500 billion in theft of trade secrets/IP, US$160 billion in data trading, US$1.6 billion of crimeware-as-a-service, and US$1 billion in ransomware. This money gets recycled, not only into more cybercrime but also into other kinds of crime, illustrating that, in the wrong hands, networks serve activities beyond the control of governments.[15]

A fourth problem is the actions taken by governments or organizations—for example, terrorist organizations—to influence the political systems or the stability of other nations. This is however beyond the scope of this book. It is a type of warfare, and does not fall within the use of social networks by individuals.

The combination of mass communication, social networks, the pressure from people in poor countries to enter developed nations, and the growing power distance may produce a new political system. The emergence of populism, nationalism and illiberal systems does not bode well for those who believe in democracy, as it will only be able to survive if it is able to solve the problems people meet in their daily lives. Through social networks, people must get rid of the "us versus them" mentality and reinstate the electorate's confidence in seeing the system as theirs.

Social networks have bestowed upon people a kind of power that has never been seen before—and now they must use it wisely. Society must seek holistic and thoughtful approaches towards protecting the use of social networks.

Social Networks—People are the Guardians

Can the internet deliver social cohesion, and can values governing free access in an environment that has primarily been "one nation, one culture, one religion" be transposed to an international world, with its many cultures, ethnicities and religions? This question explains the existential battle going on over the control of social networks, connoting that power rests with those who control and command social networks. There are three main issues.

The first issue is the question of who sets the technical standards, such as who owns the networks and who controls access to the networks. The answer is that the big internet companies run the show, such as the American "Big Five" (Apple, Alphabet, Microsoft, Facebook, and Amazon) and the Chinese "Big Three" (Baidu, Alibaba, and Tencent), with citizens and the political system out of the picture. These companies have expanded their activities beyond their core businesses. Lately, Google, Facebook and Amazon have begun to buy into submarine cables. Facebook and Amazon build their own cables to support their cloud services.

Proposition one: Introduce a high degree of transparency about who owns the networks and cables. As of now, this is no secret, but analysts need to dig—and sometimes dig deep—to discover ownership and control.

Proposition two: Strengthen anti-trust legislation by looking at how much power a company possesses in delivering a service. Most such legislation is intrasectoral, looking at a dominant market position in a particular sector or area. New attention needs to be given to the case of access to the internet and connecting people, and from an intersectoral perspective.

The second issue is the relationship between the state and the companies offering services to the people. The top ten big data corporations are in many respects more powerful than nation-states. They decide what can be transmitted via their networks. As was seen during the US presidential election in autumn 2016, such companies can allow their networks to be used in a way that certainly influenced the outcome.

The three major global powers—the United States, China, and the European Union—are each tackling this problem in their own way. The United States appears to have chosen to merge the interests of these companies with the interests of the state, which makes it difficult to distinguish the two from each other. China and the European Union have chosen to insist on state control over the data-collecting companies. The EU is using legislation to force companies to adhere to rules and regulations vis-à-vis the citizen. And China remains vigilant on the antitrust side of things by insisting that representatives of the Communist Party of China sit on the boards of these companies.

Proposition three: Democracy will be in danger if the state allows data-collecting companies to challenge its power vis-à-vis citizens. The state must be able to supervise the activity of commercial companies and be able to draw clear lines for such activities, particularly about how much personal data may be collected, public awareness about that collection process, and in some cases the state must require the consent of the citizens concerned as to whether their data may be made available to other parties.

Proposition four: An ombudsman institution (parliamentary commissioner) should be created so that citizens can inquire about the type of data private companies and government institutions have collected about them.

The third issue is how to secure information that has been put on the internet and meet the minimum standards for combating "fake news". Three things have changed the game.

The cascade effect embeds enormous power. With billions of people connected to the internet, the speed of transmission combined with the instinct of relying on first impressions gives it enormous power to shape people's mindsets and at the same time makes it extremely difficult to effectively correct false information—fake news.

Globalization changes values. The norms for what can be said publicly are not the same across the globe as they were when a dominant religion or ethnicity had controlled the norms inside a nation-state. In a national framework, nationalism or patriotism fostered unity. In a global world, it sows the seeds of division, or even conflicts.

In some cases, governments have blocked websites they consider to be "dangerous" (censorship). When interference from outside in domestic policies takes place—and the world has seen several examples of this—the government has no choice but to step in and defend the country from such attacks against its sovereignty.

For the use of social networks by citizens, the main issue is who to trust? Companies such as Facebook block certain content, but no one outside the company knows exactly what the criteria are for blocking content, nor do they know whether Facebook plays with or against the government. The game-changing element in all of this is that technology has empowered the individual to choose what news to believe in, thereby establishing a trust gap and a potential conflict vis-à-vis companies and governments shutting off access to certain websites, especially from the outside world.

Proposition five: The internet should be kept free. Any attempt to weed out fake news comes with a high risk of censorship. Still, it should be possible to exercise some kind of oversight process that results in classifying messages and marking those of dubious quality. Artificial Intelligence and Big Data may help to catch incorrect information without delay. Outside interference orchestrated by foreign governments or organizations is a different matter, and it calls for a vigorous and robust defence.

A number of countries have introduced legislation to protect against fake news. This can be done when fake news is defined as something objectively wrong or false measured against well-established facts. It is however much more difficult if fake news is perceived as deliberately misleading news on the net, which can be difficult to verify—at least in the time span needed to stop it. Even more difficult is the challenge of people in power using the net to spread news and in many cases putting forward news or points of view that are subsequently proved to be false. According to the *Washington Post*, President Trump in his first 773 days in office made 9,014 misleading or false claims.[16]

Proposition six: There is no way around entrusting social networks to people. The users of the internet must be encouraged to take an active role in repudiating fake news and flagging discriminatory or insulting messages. The issue lies in the education, literacy and gullibility of the people, not in the source of the news.

Decentralization

A tsunami of centralization has taken place in most democracies. Many small or medium-sized communities have been dissolved and replaced by larger units, which are often known as "regions". In the prism of a ministry of finance, the benefits are obvious: lower administrative expenditure. For the citizen, it means that public services and the politicians have moved further away. Power and service have grown distant.

Some decades ago, a town would have had its own hospital—perhaps not a big one, but at least a decent one. Most illnesses could be dealt with at the local level. Now, large regional hospitals have advanced and house expensive equipment designed for more complicated health cases, such as a brain tumours. This is great for those people suffering from a brain tumour, but bad for people with minor illnesses, which make up most health cases. On paper, this scenario looks great, but it amounts to a significant deterioration of facilities for most people—especially for those living in the periphery.

Proposition seven: Reverse the trend towards centralization and provide towns and local communities with facilities comparable to those that existed several decades ago. Political reform is also necessary. Local committees and mayors who can "govern" in close contact with the local people must be reinstated.

Deconcentration

The large investment funds and pension funds can be described as institutional capitalism with pro forma owners—people who have invested their money and are almost completely removed from exercising control over the disposal of their money. The number of traditional financial institutions, such as banks and savings banks, have been decimated. Those that remain have financial clout that would have been inconceivable about thirty to forty years ago.

Capitalism in its original conception—with entrepreneurs saving, investing their money and building factories—no longer exists. Almost all economic operators are controlled by a network of funds and non-transparent cross-ownership.

Transparency is sorely lacking with regard to cross-ownership, making it difficult to fully estimate the financial—and probably also political—power held in the hands not only of the companies engaged in cross-ownership but also of the people controlling them, who in reality are shuffling around the savings of the global population.

Proposition eight: There should be much stronger awareness of the ownership by companies of the shares in other companies, and in case of mergers and acquisitions whether institutional investors sit on the board of both companies involved.

Activation of Corporate Social Responsibility

Corporate social responsibility (CSR) has grown to be an important aspect of most companies, but it is unclear whether corporations see themselves as platforms or as stakeholders in society.

Many CSR activities take the form of grants for various social activities, such as the arts or sports. This is commendable, but CSR should go much further than that. The purpose of business is to deliver goods and services to society more than earning a profit. The business world gains from being part of society and by offering services that are indispensable for business activities, such as education, transportation and health. Businesses should see "paying back" to society as their main objective.

Globalization has cut the link between businesses and local communities. Companies relocate, seeking to operate in countries not only where costs are lower but where it is most profitable. And they use existing tax systems to register activities and profits in countries with the lowest tax rates.

Proposition nine: The public should take a much stronger interest in whether corporations see their CSR role as a stakeholder in society. The iron law of responsibility says that "In the long run, those who do not use power in a manner that society considers responsible will tend to lose it." But this only works if citizens actively let corporations know what "society considers responsible".

More Fairness, Reduce Inequality, Increase Social Mobility

Social mobility rose in most democracies during the first seventy-five years or so of the twentieth century, but has since stalled or regressed. Sociological studies conducted in the United States have revealed that people are either well off and well educated and that their children will be in the same social strata, or that they are not, and that there is little chance for them or their children to move upwards. The victim is meritocracy.

This is because of growing inequality that makes it prohibitively expensive for families with a lower income to fund enrolment in top schools and top universities for their children. It also reflects the deepening gap between those who constitute the elite, in a broad sense, and those who do not. Insurmountable barriers between these social groups mean that those who are not in the top social strata feel that society is unfair and is not giving them and their children a chance. Skills seem to be a decisive factor in generating income inequality.

The effect is a feeling of being left out, which nurtures discontent and which in the long run will threaten the cohesion of societies and nation-states, removing the sense of being part of the same community. Economically, it is an enormous waste, as the mass of talent is not being fully used.

Proposition ten: Steps should be taken towards providing access to the best schools to anybody who is qualified to attend them. Government grants or tuition fee policies should be implemented to ensure that all qualified students have access to the best universities. It is very much up to governments to step in and enhance social mobility.

Proposition eleven: A new social contract needs to be written. The points to focus on should be to balance between what citizens do for society, how much they rely on society, their political influence, how increased wealth is distributed among citizens, and how those citizens use that wealth—including how much is channelled back to support social activities.

Democracy at Risk

Combining the elements outlined above, two issues stand out as the main risks to democracy or, to put it more broadly, good governance.

The first is eroding trust in governments and authorities.

Over sixty years, the share of Americans who say they can trust their government to do the right thing has fallen from 73 per cent to 17 per cent, with only 3 per cent saying *always* and 14 per cent saying *most of the time*.[17]

A poll covering twenty-seven countries reveals that 51 per cent are dissatisfied with the way democracy works, with a minority of 45 per cent being satisfied. Large majorities of Italians, Spaniards and Greeks are dissatisfied, and even in countries like Sweden and The Netherlands, where you would think democracy was firmly entrenched, more than 60 per cent were dissatisfied.[18]

In a post on LinkedIn on 20 March 2018, Bryan Druzin revealed that the percentage of those "believing it is essential to live in a democracy" had fallen from the 1930s to the 1980s in the United States from about 75 per cent to about 30 per cent, and in Britain from about 70 per cent to about 30 per cent.

There are certainly several reasons behind this development. One is that democracies have failed to deliver solutions to the major problems, where those of immigration and refugees probably stand out. Secondly, the global financial crisis cast doubts over the strength of the economy, but even more crucially conveyed an impression of inequality and unfairness. Thirdly, the increasing dehumanization of the public sector, with contact between citizens and local officials being replaced by digitalization, may also play a role, as formerly a citizen's contact with officials conveyed a strong element of trust, which digitalization can never give.

The second reason is the explosive rise of social networks that have sown confusion and uncertainty about what is right or wrong, permissible or forbidden, and blurring the distinction between fact and fake news.

In the real world, social networks may be the crucial element in eroding trust between governments and local communities, as their use leaves many citizens baffled and questioning the government. They are bombarded with news and information from so many sources that it is impossible for them to distinguish between what is the truth and what is not.

The main factor in regaining trust for governments might not be to introduce control, however tempting this might at first look and however well it might work. Control and censorship can turn social networks into an authoritarian venue. It also raises a good deal of questions about who is in control, particularly if the control/censorship is exercised by private companies. Unregulated freedom creates a platform for free speech and stimulates innovation, but it also opens the door for "fake news". Someone must design a system that opens the door for the benefits but which shuts the door on the risks.

Such a system must be designed by the citizens because they are the main users of the internet and they will suffer the most if it comes under authoritarian control or if it is dominated by fake news. Social networks have bestowed upon people a type of power that has never been seen before—except perhaps in Greek city states some 2,500 years ago—and now they must use it wisely. They must create instruments that are capable of tackling centralization, concentration, corporate social responsibility, fairness and social mobility.

Key Points

The failure of democracy to respond to challenges and to deliver results has invariably had repercussions for the role of the nation-state, even if there is no direct link between democracy as a political system and the nation-state.

But the growing weakness, perplexity and irresoluteness of democracy imply that what might still be classified as leading nation-states (the United States, with a system often labelled dysfunctional, and Britain in political chaos after Brexit) are unable to tackle a whole new string of problems associated with new technology and its impact on the human mindset.

The most important issue may be the coming power game between the state—not necessarily the nation-state—and the big data companies encroaching on what used to be the exclusive rights of the state.

Notes

1. This chapter is an updated and amended version of three articles published on the website of The National Interest, 11 December 2018, 22 January 2019 and 11 March 2019.
2. https://www.bbc.com/news/uk-politics-38762034.
3. Claire Wardle, "A New World Disorder", *Scientific American* (September 2019): 82–87.
4. Analyses of Adolf Hitler's speeches reveal that this was exactly how he seduced his audience.
5. See, for example, Anil K. Seth, "Our Inner Universe", *Scientific American* (September 2019): 34–41.
6. UN population statistics.
7. https://www.oecd.org/els/mig/migration-policy-debates-13.pdf.
8. https://www.independent.co.uk/news/uk/politics/eu-workers-uk-tax-treasury-brexit-migrants-british-citizens-a8542506.html.
9. https://www.independent.co.uk/news/uk/politics/eu-workers-uk-tax-treasury-brexit-migrants-british-citizens-a8542506.html.
10. First published 1949.
11. Anne T. Lawrence and James Weber, *Business and Society*, 15th ed. (New York: McGraw-Hill, 2017).
12. Ibid.

13. http://www.bbc.com/capital/story/20190108-how-long-it-takes-a-ceo-to-earn-more-than-you-do-in-a-year.
14. https://www.nydailynews.com/news/politics/cost-u-s-senate-seat-10-5-million-article-.1.1285491tps://researchbriefings.parliament.uk/ResearchBriefing/Summary/SN05125.
15. "Web of Profit". 2018. Bromium.com/cybercrime.
16. https://www.washingtonpost.com/politics/2019/03/04/president-trump-has-made-false-or-misleading-claims-over-days/?utm_term=.b2968c32e506.
17. https://www.people-press.org/2019/04/11/public-trust-in-government-1958-2019/.
18. https://www.pewresearch.org/global/2019/04/29/many-across-the-globe-are-dissatisfied-with-how-democracy-is-working/.

4

The Nation-State[1]

Like democracy, the nation-state is under attack. This should not come as a surprise as democracy is in many respects the political system born to support the nation-state. Like democracy, the strength of the nation-state is, or rather was, coherence, solidarity and a feeling among citizens of being in the same boat. Under the impact of information and communication technology, citizens shift their allegiance to other institutions or groups, cutting the link of mutual dependence holding the nation-state together.

- It is being replaced by people shifting their adherence and loyalty from a nation-state (nationality as identity) to common and shared values.
- The role of migration questions the prerogative of the nation-state as the "best" political system. Migration is rarely motivated by a wish to take on another national identity.
- It is being undermined by the big data companies delivering instruments for communication—social networks overruling the privilege of a nation-state of controlling communication with its people.

A genuine nation-state with a single ethnicity, a single religion and a common culture is difficult to find nowadays. Fifty years ago, such could perhaps be found among the Nordic countries in Europe (Sweden, Denmark, Norway, Finland and Iceland), but since migration began in the 1970s and 1980s the picture has changed.

And with regard to the idea of the nation-state, it should be borne in mind that even if the label is used freely for countries around the globe, there is in reality a big difference among nation-states depending on where they find themselves and their history.

Almost all the genuine nation-states are to be found in Europe. The idea of the nation-state goes back to the end of the Thirty Years War with the Westphalian Peace in 1648. Over recent decades, minorities have risen to question their adherence to the nation-state, as seen in Britain with Scotland and in Spain with Catalonia. It is sometimes forgotten that two instances of what look like solid European nation-states—Germany and Italy—were first created in 1871 and 1861, respectively. In the early 1990s, Yugoslavia, an artificial nation-state created after the end of World War I, collapsed.

North America offers an example of a nation-state formed by migration, mainly from its former colonial master (Britain) and then from Europe. By self-proclaimed ancestry, the largest group in the United States is that citing German ancestry (44 million), followed by those citing Irish and English ancestries, which goes to show how diverse the United States is as a nation-state.[2]

Latin America saw the nation-state emerge following decolonization about two hundred years ago, and the populations now represent a mixture of the people living there prior to colonialization with migrants from the former colonial powers and from Europe.

In Asia, the nation-state is something new that came about as a result of decolonialization, with former colonies transformed into nation-states. The three Asian giants—China, Japan and India—are all registered as nation-states, but history tells us that each of them had their own way of getting there: Japan as an island nation; China as an old empire with a large group of minorities and a tradition of the periphery fighting the centre;[3] India only became a nation-state in political terms in 1947 after the British left.

Africa and the Middle East have to a large extent been shaped by the former colonial powers that had divided ancient kingdoms and tribes, first into spheres of interest and then into colonies to be exploited. In many cases, political borders isolate ancient traditions and separate people who used to live adjacent to one another.

In the discussion that follows, the focus will be on the nation-state in Asia, and primarily on China, as the area where the future power game is taking place.

An Emerging, New World View—A Shift of Paradigm

The age of enlightenment is coming to an end. Isaac Asimov hit the nail on the head when he said "Anti-intellectualism has been a constant thread winding its way through our political and cultural life, nurtured by the false notion that democracy means that *'my ignorance is just as good as your knowledge'*".[4]

The behaviour of people is no longer primarily controlled by reason; it is therefore more difficult to predict and to be influenced by policymakers. The fact of the 2017 Nobel Prize for Economics being awarded to Richard Thaler is both praiseworthy and lamentable at the same time. Praiseworthy for recognizing that economics built around rationality does not reflect human behaviour. And lamentable that it took the science of economics so long to recognize this.

Once people have made up their minds on the basis of emotion, intuition and instinct, they cannot be swayed by rationality and logic. Even if someone else can prove to them that their position is based on a fallacy, people will stick to their original posture; they may even harden it.

Social networks do not work to deepen and strengthen coherence and mutual respect. They in fact do the contrary. People are reinforced in their initial beliefs because those who react to them are of like mind. We communicate more and more with people who hold the same opinion and less and less with people who hold different views.

It becomes difficult to govern countries from the centre with compromises and consensus. The feeling is that, increasingly, the situation is "them" versus "us".

Superficiality is the companion of subjectivity. When no arguments or facts are required, why bother to provide evidence for statements and positions. Just hurl out accusations or praise inside 340 words!

The words *alternative facts* should make you shudder. Facts are facts. Or are they? The consequence is that facts can be and are disputed. How can governments govern when facts are not acknowledged?

The tendency towards splitting societies and allowing extremist views signifies the end of what used to be a civilized debate. Honesty and integrity disappear, yielding ground to the stubborn defence of views that disregard facts and objectivity.

The established global system is built around nation-states. It is losing because it is a political instrument tailor-made to an epoch of civilization: industrialization and the age of economics. As that epoch is petering out, so is the nation-state. Britain and Spain face regions wanting to secede. The Soviet Union fell apart in 1991. In the United States, California flirts with secession. The feud between California and the Trump administration over vehicle-emission standards has now got to the point that the state of California is suing federal agencies.[5]

These trends are changing the framework for globalization with phenomenal speed and are introducing unpredictability.

The smooth function of the global system presupposes and depends on actions and messages, whether made openly or discreetly, signalling intentions. Such behaviour serves to contain crises and prevent escalation. But signalling is only effective if there is a common rule book acknowledged by everybody, making the interpretation of signals easy—you know what the other party means and the other party knows that you know!

Over the last decade or two, the common rule book has been torn up. No common interpretation exists anymore. The tweets of President Trump leave other countries perplexed and even aghast. The global institutional system is crumbling. The United Nations and its Security Council no longer serves as a forum for negotiation. The World Trade Organization has lost its role as the upholder of global trade rules. The International Monetary Fund and the World Bank do not represent a common international economic policy. Voting rights are out of tune with the weights of countries in the global economy as emerging markets and developing countries are grossly under-represented.

The introduction of a coalition of the willing as some kind of replacement sounds good, but what about the unwilling?

With the economic model of capitalism—globalization—technology still delivers high economic growth lifting millions out of poverty, but external social diseconomies have taken on a magnitude that threatens the model.

Instead of cooperating with nation-states to create employment, multinational companies shuffle financial transactions around. The wage share has fallen dramatically in almost all the major industrialized countries. Local plants have disappeared leaving once-thriving towns deserted. Technology demands new skills that the education system is unable to foresee, resulting in a mismatch between the supply and demand of skills.

In industrial countries, the privileged class of skilled workers in manufacturing lose their jobs. They used to be the core of economic life and had constituted an important share of the middle class, which stabilized political life. Now they have suddenly found themselves in the role of social losers. Globalization brings with it large-scale migration motivated by economic factors. People are confronted with neighbours who adhere to a different culture. Paradoxically, this makes them question their own identity.

The underlying trend of scepticism about the virtues of globalization tells us that it has gone too far, too fast and too deep. The situation could have been dealt with by domestic policies as a counterweight to the negative side-effects (external diseconomies) of globalization, but few nation-states have been able to find the right balance between globalization and domestic policies. The result has been that benefits are spread in an inequitable way. Policymakers do not seem to have grasped that people have begun to prioritize human, social and economic security, and have downgraded (but not rejected) economic gains.

Turning to China, we can see that the Communist Party of China (CPC) seems to be well aware of this shift.

On 9 January 2017, Bloomberg reported that as China's top leaders tallied the cost of another year of debt-fuelled growth, the imperative for stability as a leadership reshuffle loomed later in the year prompted an unexpected conclusion. The price was too high, the leaders agreed. The accumulation of debt used to fuel smokestack industries from steel to cement had helped win the short-term battle for growth, but the triumph itself undermined the foundations of long-term expansion. What followed was an order to central and local government officials that if this year they are forced to choose, *stability must be the priority*,[6] and everything else, including the growth target and economic reform, would be secondary.[7]

China has entered globalization to take a leading role at the moment the United States and Britain are questioning the system. This creates problems and an opportunity. Problems in the form of unpredictability. And the opportunity to step into the vacuum and to shape things—in effect to become a leader. Leadership is about exercising power without abusing it, and without antagonizing other countries.

An Outline of the Coming Power Game

The power game is normally seen as competition among nation-states and to often be about possession of territory. This is the Westphalian picture the world has been boxed into since the end of the Thirty Years War that haunted Europe between 1618 and 1648. It has been refined by von Clausewitz, with his famous dictum that war is the continuation of politics with other means.[8]

Following in the wake of this paradigm, a great deal of intellectual efforts, political thinking and military planning has been devoted to the Thucydides trap.[9] The main theory of this is that a declining superpower will watch with anxiety a growing competitor, contemplating whether it is in its interest to launch a preventive war whilst still in a position to win it, or to wait and to risk losing its position of superiority.

This way of thinking reflects a worldview where military power is the predominant power vector. Today, the projection of power is composed of a triad: military strength, economics/finance, and persuasion/perception.

Since 1945, very few wars have produced the results that were looked for. The list of stalemates or outright defeats for those who sought to intervene are long: the Korean War, France in Indochina, the United States in Vietnam, Britain and France in Egypt over the Suez Canal, the Soviet Union in Afghanistan, the United States in Iraq and Afghanistan in 2003. Only the efforts of the US-led coalition in the first Gulf War of 1991 can be classified as a "victory", and that was because of restraint and a limited, well-defined objective.

Economics and finance have served as effective levers of power for the United States. But, as US economic power declines, so does its effectiveness in this regard. In fact, economics and finance have been linked to the power and clout of the United States as by far the most important nation—the indispensable nation-state in the sense that very few if any other nation-states could do without the United States.

Some observers take the view that the United States and China should look (and perhaps they are doing this) for a kind of *economic* power-sharing, by piggy backing on each other to form an economic growth machine. Such a model makes a lot of sense, but it neglects the fact that the main players in economic globalization are multinational companies, and not nation-states. Of total sales made by companies on the Standard & Poor's 500 list, 44.4 per cent come from abroad. Companies on the list with more than half of sales abroad registered a rise in profit of 21 per cent, more than double of those dependent on the home market.[10]

Today's global supply chain means that, for example, American multinational companies cannot function without access to the global market, and in particular the Chinese market, for the purposes of production and sales. These companies buy a large proportion of the components they use from China, and they rely on manufacturing in China. Research shows that the list of suppliers for Apple stretches to more than two hundred all across the globe.[11]

The global supply chain links multinational companies to each other, and this has reached such a level that it makes war or a large-scale military conflict impossible. This is one of the reasons that the military power vector has been weakened. A similar view was conventional wisdom prior to World War I.[12] The difference is that in those days economic globalization was confined to trade, and the global supply chain as seen today did not exist. American and British multinationals were not dependent on components manufactured abroad.

There may be many reasons explaining the American withdrawal from participating in the formation of the Trans Pacific Partnership (TPP), but one of them is certainly that multinational companies headquartered in the United States have a large share of their activities (revenue and profit) abroad, allowing them to operate without any dependence on which nation-state or group of nation-states sets the rules (norms and technical standards). There is no academic analysis with supporting evidence, but perhaps multinational companies find life better without a trade pact like the TPP (and you can add to this the equivalent initiative from across the Atlantic, the TTIP), giving them room to manoeuvre and leaving them to set their own rules.

The most interesting aspects to Chinese overseas investment are that:

- China has created multinational companies mainly through its sovereign wealth fund (the Chinese Investment Corporation, or CIC) and state-owned enterprises, in addition to, albeit to a lesser extent, private companies; and
- the fact of the large data companies: Baidu, Alibaba and Tencent.

These aspect both illustrate two main points:

1. China's economic model and business system are "Chinese", and they cannot be measured or judged by traditional Western yardsticks. China is operating inside its own framework that has been forged by centuries of evolution, and it intends to develop and adopt a model of its own.[13] In case any doubts had persisted, President Xi Jinping removed them at the Nineteenth Party Congress when he said, "It [China's business model] offers a new option for other countries and nations who want to speed up their development while preserving their independence".[14]
2. China needs access to economic globalization to maintain momentum for economic growth. Obstacles to this are casting doubt over whether China can rely on the existing system as a framework for going global to support the economic growth necessary for the further development of the country.

Economic globalization is turning into the biggest power game the world has ever seen. It will not be conducted along Westphalian lines—nation-state versus nation-state—but between large multinational companies, particularly the data companies, and the state.

The power of multinational enterprises can be illustrated by mentioning that of nearly six thousand of the world's largest public and private firms, just the top 10 per cent captured 80 per cent of the profits. The list of those 10 per cent includes not only the well-known American and European enterprises but also reveals the economic power of emerging markets and developing economies. In the late 1990s, American companies accounted for 45 per cent of this select group of companies—now they only represent 38 per cent. Companies from China, India, Japan and Korea have increased their share, going up from 7 per cent to 22 per cent. Another noteworthy point, especially when looking at the impact of digitalization on the power structure, is that a number of enterprises that were unknown a decade ago, like Alibaba, Facebook and Tencent—all operating in the digital world, and especially in social networks—are on the list.[15]

The Coming Power Game: Multinational Companies

The main change to the event over preceding decades has been the emergence of multinational companies from Asia and in particular from China.

An important player among sovereign wealth funds is the Chinese Investment Corporation (CIC), which has investments abroad that run close to US$1 trillion,[16] or perhaps more. It had originally focused its attention on resources such as oil and gas (energy) and the financial system. The corporation's investments in the Western financial system are especially interesting, as CIC took large losses through the global financial crises, whilst on the other hand the move offered it the opportunity to buy into Western financial institutions, and subsequently allowing it to shuffle China's savings surplus around. The Western institutions had conducted their activities largely according to their own interests. China came to think that perhaps it would be better if such things were done according to its own interests. This required an ownership stake and a long-term process of setting up its own financial institutions. Later, the CIC diversified into various economic sectors, including agriculture, manufacturing and advanced technologies. One of the underlying purposes has been to acquire knowledge and skills about how to manage a multinational company.

The policy imperative for China's rulers is political and social stability. History has taught us without any mercy that social instability has been the bane of many dynasties and has created turmoil for several rulers. To avoid this situation, jobs need to be offered, and this requires high economic growth. As China's economy enters a slower trajectory, albeit one still with an enviable growth rate, the country has to look abroad, and hence the need to build multinational companies. The finance is available, but neither the management skills nor the technological know-how are. Such skills can be built over time, but time is precious for China's political leaders, and they are seeking to take the shortcut of acquiring companies from around the world.

A case in point was the purchase by China of Sweden's Volvo—a car manufacturer with a good brand and reputation, which for some years was recognized as a world leader in safety, and which is well entrenched in many important global markets. Ownership of Volvo offers China at least two things: insight in managing a global car manufacturer with a global supply chain, and customers in many markets. Diversity and adaptability are the keywords in this.

China's economic structure, with its sovereign wealth funds and state-owned enterprises, offers an opportunity to spread the lessons and skills obtained beyond the immediate investor, contrary to the case with Western investments, which would invariably be undertaken by a single company that would pay for and keep the skills it acquired for itself. The other side of the coin is that many Western nations that see domestic enterprises being bought by "China" worry that mergers and acquisitions are being undertaken precisely to acquire skills, and not for any considerations of a market economy context where the investment would be profitable for the company.

There are three kinds of barriers embedded in the existing global system that confronts China.

The first is that it is more difficult than presumed to go from the national market to the international market and later to the global one.

An awareness of cultural (behavioural) differences needs to be factored in. The British and later the Americans shaped the system so other countries and markets had to adjust to them. Chinese companies must adjust to the British/American behavioural pattern. That has proved to be difficult. Furthermore, Chinese investments are beginning to be made in some countries that have expressed vocal public opinions that are unwelcoming. In Vietnam, a scheme for bauxite mining in the Central highlands involving Chinese companies, potentially amounting up to US$15 billion, encountered stiff resistance, partly out of concern for ethnic minorities living there and partly because of historical animosity between Vietnam and its northern neighbour. Interestingly, one of the "dissidents" was a hero from the wars against France and the United States, General Vo Nguyen Giap.[17]

Chinese companies are not used to incorporating public opinion into policymaking, and if they are the normal reaction is that investment coming "our" way is good. A broader concern for the quality of life of the people living at the site where investments take place is less widespread among Chinese companies, not having encountered such grass-roots movements at home. Corporate social responsibility is taught in China, but applying it when starting to operate abroad is something else, and much more demanding.

The second barrier is the Chinese policy of decoupling investments from domestic policies in the recipient country (hands-off). China has apparently reaped some success among emerging markets and developing economies as many governments have felt annoyed at Western countries harping on about human rights. The matter, however, is not only about human rights. Attitudes towards corruption and kick-backs may also play a role.

Industrialized countries signed in 1997 the OECD Convention on Combating Bribery of Foreign Public Officials in International Business Transactions.[18] It entered into force in 1999 and eight non-OECD member states joined (China was not among them), bringing the total number of signatories to forty-three. Since then, the convention has been supplemented with recommendations. For China, this raises the question of its status in international or global corporate governance. Does the country's non-signatory status mean that China allows bribery? The campaign inside China to bring corruption and bribery under control indicates knowledge that corruption distorts the economy—the price mechanism is not allowed to steer the allocation of production factors. The result is lower growth.

The burden of a superpower to provide protection for its assets and citizens abroad has not yet come to China, even if its overseas assets are rapidly increasing. Foreign and security policy need to be considered, as had been the case for the United States and Britain. Both these nations learned the hard way the cost of nationalization of investments abroad and citizens left stranded, even in some cases seeing their investments subjugated by a new regime that broke the promises of the earlier regime.

This reality is dawning on China.[19] One of the first cases took place in Libya, from where, after the fall of Colonel Gaddafi and the subsequent turmoil, China had to evacuate a large number of its citizens. If China does not have the capability and willingness to step in, Chinese citizens working for Chinese companies or taking part in investment projects will not be safe. Chinese assets can be confiscated. A policy of non-interference cannot be reconciled with a strong role in globalization. The question for China is whether there is another way than gradually being pushed towards a policy similar to the one adopted by the United States. Whatever China chooses, the realities will speak loudly, and this puts the basic question of China's role in economic globalization squarely on the agenda of policymakers.

China's overseas direct investments are far from as gigantic as some observers have described them. They are rising fast, but they are not yet comparable to those of the United States or the European Union (with or without Britain).

The third barrier is growing Western anxiety about China buying into strategic industries, whatever that means.

Western countries did not have any worries of losing control over resources or of threats to national security when other Western countries invested in them. Most of these countries were partners in a military alliance (NATO) or close allies of the United States. But the situation is not the same when China enters the game. Not only is China a newcomer, and perhaps not fully aware of the written and unwritten rules, but Western countries fear that China harbours long-term ambitions of gaining control over their natural resources or transferring technology, and ultimately harming their national interests.

Rarely is it said openly that the only difference now is that it is China that is doing it—after Britain and the United States had done it for one or two centuries. The reason for this silence is that it would disclose a global system operating under a kind of double standard, which in fact it does, but it is not supposed to.

In Australia, the saga of Kidston cattle station—Australia's largest—had been going on for some time, as the government had blocked its sale to a Chinese investor. The story ended in December 2016 with Australia's richest woman, Gina Rinehart, buying two thirds and a Chinese investor taking a minority share of a third of S. Kidman & Co. The Australian treasurer stated openly that "I have decided that the acquisition of Kidman as proposed would not be contrary to the national interest and will be permitted to proceed."[20]

After more than half a year of uncertainty, the Canadian government in February 2013 approved the purchase by CNOOC of the oil and gas company Nexen, but only after having pledged this to be the last one of its kind and having achieved clearance from the US Committee on Foreign Investment on account of Nexen's operations in the Gulf of Mexico. In fact, a couple of years earlier, the United States had rejected the purchase by CNOOC of an American oil and gas company, Unocal, invoking national security concerns. Both Nexen and Unocal are fairly large companies, but not giants.[21]

In September 2017, President Trump blocked the purchase of Lattice Semiconductor Corporation, explaining "The national-security risk posed by the transaction relates to, among other things, the potential transfer of intellectual property to the foreign acquirer, the Chinese government's role in supporting this transaction, the importance of semiconductor supply chain integrity to the United States Government, and the use of Lattice products by the United States Government."[22]

In Europe, the German government blocked the sale of Kuka, an industrial robot maker, raising concerns about the transfer of technology deemed to be important for Germany's competitive advantage in this sector. The sale of Aixtron, a chip equipment maker, was blocked by the German government for national security reasons. In Britain, Prime Minister Theresa May in summer 2016 temporarily blocked the project for the construction of Hinkley Point C nuclear power station, which is partly financed by China, allegedly because of Britain's energy security considerations. The European Commission is, at the behest of several member states, preparing a scheme to scrutinize investments from third countries in strategic sectors. Nobody involved has specifically mentioned China, but there is no doubt that it will be mainly, although not exclusively, China who would be the target of such a scheme if or when it is approved.[23]

To these three points must be added that *China itself* is reconsidering the role of overseas mergers and acquisitions. For 2016, Chinese overseas mergers and acquisitions amounted to US$246 billion—a remarkable figure by any measure. According to Bloomberg, however, the amount was down by 67 per cent for the first four months of 2017.[24] The reason for this is not to be found in economics or business practices, but in deliberate restrictions or, rather, guidance rolled out by the Chinese authorities (the National Development and Reform Commission and the

State Council).[25] Overseas investments are classified into three categories. The category of banned investment includes gambling and core military equipment. Property, sport, and entertainment falls into the "restricted" category, which means such investments will undergo close scrutiny and will presumably only receive approval if good arguments can be presented. Investments in property are estimated to have reached around US$30 billion by 2016, perhaps more, as statistics for private residential investments may not be reliable.[26] The third category is encouraged, which aims at infrastructure projects, in particular those supporting the Belt and Road Initiative.

The actions taken may also have been influenced by efforts to manage the exchange rate and prevent businessmen and officials circumventing efforts to reduce corruption. It seems however that the core reason has been the drive to channel overseas investment into sectors and enterprises of importance to China for the development of its role in economic globalization, as seen and defined by the political leadership.

Suffice it to say that China's political leaders have concluded that the country can no longer afford what may be termed "sterile" overseas investments; i.e., investments that may be good for a company but not for China. Buying property may provide a good yield for the investor, but it will not bring home know-how or other benefits useful in economic globalization. A more strategic approach is called for, by focusing on what may be termed "societal" benefits, with investments scrutinized and selected according to their overall significance for China.

The big data companies play a special role because they possess and use the new and strongest future power parameter: persuasion and the shaping of perceptions.

The Coming Power Game: Data Companies versus the State

The big data companies over the last twenty years have collected an amazing array of information about individuals and companies. Obviously, they use this in their business activities and, equally obviously, they intrude into privacy by doing so. People and companies are not informed about what information concerning them has been stored and who has access to it.

As of 2017, the world has seven such companies, with a couple more on the fringes. China is home to Baidu, Alibaba and Tencent. The United States is home to Google (company name Alphabet), Apple, Facebook and Amazon.

Microsoft can also be added to this list. The purchase by Microsoft of LinkedIn in 2016 for US$26 billion serves as an example of the power of these companies. LinkedIn is a network of more than 433 million highly professional people.[27] They communicate with one another; they seek jobs; they "brag" about performances, successes and achievements; they exchange information about their ambitions and plans; and they share their ideas. Microsoft has tapped into what is the global intellectual elite.

At first glance the reaction might be "so what?" But the insights obtained provide a unique opportunity to discern how business is developing, what new ideas are being presented, what is on the crest of the wave and what is falling out of fashion. Microsoft can tap into this enormous pool of knowledge and see sooner than almost anybody else the direction of global business. In a power game scenario, it will know more than the governments do. Governments may well launch large R&D programmes, but they are actually not as well-positioned as Microsoft in being able to guess where the money should be spent.

With respect to potential competitors, once it learns about new companies that are developing competing products, Microsoft can step in and buy these upstarts. It can then either incorporate the new technology into its own line of products or kill off those it deems a risk to its own product lines. Legally, there may be no objections or concerns about this, but in a power game scenario—it gives such a company enormous clout. According to Franklin Foer (author of *World Without Mind: The Existential Threat of Big Tech*), "in Silicon Valley, the greatest ambition now is not to displace Google or Facebook. It's to get bought by Google and Facebook."[28]

Traffic on the internet is of course not random, but is steered by algorithms. No one knows how prominent a role a specific piece of information is given. It may depend on the relevant person's use of LinkedIn, or it may depend on some other criteria chosen by Microsoft. It is wrong to use the word *censorship*, in the same way that it would be wrong to say a newspaper editor choosing not to run an article is exercising censorship, but the power to decide is priceless.

In the industrial age, governments have provided much of the infrastructure that is used by the business sector. For many decades, telephone and telegraph services came totally or partly under government control; in many countries, concessionary companies operated as a kind of right hand for the government.

Nation-states and governments have surrendered control of the infrastructure for transmitting information and communication and have handed it over to the same group of companies that control what is transmitted over the internet. A near monopoly for global communication is invested in less than ten companies.

Facebook, Microsoft and Spain's telecom company Telxius have built a gigantic cable connecting Virginia in the United States to Bilbao in Spain that has a mind-boggling capacity of 160 terabits per second of bandwidth. Facebook and Google, along with Pacific Light Data Communication from Hong Kong, is building an 8,000-mile cable under the Pacific that will have an unrivalled capacity. Google, linking up with Indosat Ooredoo, Singtel, Subpartners and Telstra, connects Singapore with Perth and Sydney with a cable that has a capacity of 16 terabits per second.[29]

The financial power possessed by the large multinational companies is terrifying. According to Thomson Reuters, five of the largest multinational companies sit on cash reserves of US$5.1 trillion, which is close to a third of US GDP. American corporations command US$2 trillion. The so-called "formidable five data companies" have a market capitalization of just below US$3 trillion (close to a sixth of US GDP). They have US$400 billion in cash at their disposal, ranked in order of the cash holdings as follows: Apple, Google (Alphabet), Microsoft, Facebook, and Amazon. This figure is just below that of the GDP of Belgium,[30] and about 80 per cent of total US gross domestic expenditure on R&D (2015 figures).[31] Apple's spending on R&D runs to about US$10 billion,[32] which looks sizeable until you compare it to the cash pile it has of more than twenty times that amount. Apparently, the big data companies, like their companions in the business sector, do not expect to pour money into research, but prefer to have a "war chest" to boost their standing in the power game.

China's Alibaba and Tencent have a combined market capitalization of about US$700 billion and free cash flows of about RMB125 billion, which is equivalent to about US$80 billion.[33] These figures seem paltry compared to their American "cousins", with a combined market capitalization of about 85 per cent that of Apple's and 3.5 per cent of China's GDP. But, bearing in mind how fast they got there, it does not take much imagination to envisage the enormous sums ahead of us. Even if both absolute figures and shares of GDP disclose stronger and bigger American companies, the growth prospects of China's big three augur a certain degree of financial clout in just a few years' time that could cause concern for the government/CPC. Over the last ten years, Tencent's free cash flow has increased eighty-two times to RMB61 billion,[34] and Alibaba's fifty-five times to RMB73 billion.[35]

Governments can basically choose between three options: do nothing (close your eyes), merge with the companies, or confront the companies.

The United States seems to be considering the option of a mutually beneficial relationship (merge). We continually hear stories of how US intelligence gets access to data collected by the big companies. In 2013 the *Washington Post* reported that a programme codenamed PRISM under the National Security Agency (NSA) and the Federal Bureau of Investigation (FBI) got access to Microsoft, Yahoo, Google, Facebook, PalTalk, AOL, Skype, YouTube, and Apple. The story was controversial and it triggered a debate over whether it was accurate, during which the director of the NSA stated that only people outside the United States had been targeted, which in the context of globalization makes it worse. Google responded by saying: "Google cares deeply about the security of our users' data." A spokesman for the company continued, "We disclose user data to government in accordance with the law, and we review all such requests carefully. From time to time, people allege that we have created a government 'back door' into our systems, but Google does not have a 'back door' for the government to access private user data." Microsoft weighed in saying, "We provide customer data only when we receive a legally binding order or subpoena to do so, and never on a voluntary basis. In addition, we only ever comply with orders for requests about specific accounts or identifiers. If the government has a broader voluntary national security program to gather customer data we don't participate in it."[36]

Knowingly or not, US government policy has favoured the rapid expansion of companies that collect data for their own private use in a market economy framework, and the government has come to realize that this represents a trove of information of vital importance for national security.

The United States illustrates the approach of not confronting these companies or bringing them under government control, but rather to investigate the limits whereby the state can use the information garnered by the companies. The US attitude is apparently that companies with a deep knowledge about citizens, companies and the exchange of information and views do not constitute a threat to the state. Perhaps some kind of "mutual integration", seeing the data companies and the government moving closer, blurring the separation between government agencies and private enterprise is possible. The US tradition of and respect for the business sector, combined with the traditionally weak state, might open the door for such a model, which would be unthinkable in many other countries. The prospect of using data companies in a future power game of economic globalization could be tempting for the United States, which is registering a weakening of its overall economic position that has to be compensated for.

The European Union has no big data companies, which may explain why its member countries see the situation of such companies and the state in an adversarial context. Another and perhaps more important reason is the awareness among Europeans about privacy. A third explanation alleges that US data companies shuffle revenue and profits around, in some cases playing governments against one another, in order to seek benefits such as low taxes or similar economic help.

Whatever may be the reason, Europe has mapped a course clearly indicating a wish to bring the data companies under state/government control. In July 2016 the European Commission adopted the EU-US privacy shield. According to the commission, "This new framework protects the fundamental rights of anyone in the EU whose personal data is transferred to the United States as well as bringing legal clarity for businesses relying on transatlantic data transfers. The new arrangement includes: strong data protection obligations on companies receiving personal data from the EU, safeguards on U.S. government access to data, effective protection and redress for individuals, annual joint review to monitor the implementation."[37]

The rules for the transfer of data outside the European Union is stricter after EU-regulation 2016/679 entered into force in May 2018.

The regulation means that European businesses will need to be aware of where their data is stored; if it is outside the EU, they are required to ensure the data is treated and transferred according to EU rules.[38]

The European Commission has adopted an aggressive line in investigating tax payments by large American companies. In August 2016 the European Commission asked Ireland to recover 13 billion euros given to Apple and regarded by the European Commission as illegal state aid. When Ireland did not comply, the Commission took the case to the European Court of Justice.[39] According to media reports, analogous such cases are in the pipeline involving Google and Amazon. This is unquestioningly entering a complicated legal ruleset, but the interesting aspect is the political will that has been demonstrated in bringing these companies under control and forcing them not to look for state aid in trying to exploit the benefits of the single market.

China is home to Baidu, Alibaba and Tencent, but it is difficult for an outsider to gauge the exact relationship between these companies and the government, or rather the CPC. Many Western observers jump to the conclusion that efforts to bring them under control are because of censorship or are linked to making life difficult for overseas data companies, implicitly favouring Chinese companies who know how to manoeuvre in the Chinese political and regulatory environment. Both reasons may be true up to a point.

In September 2017, Tencent, Baidu and Sina were fined for violating the Cybersecurity Law.[40] The authorities stated that the companies had failed to properly manage their social media platforms, allowing some of their users to "spread information of violence and terror, false rumours, pornography, and other information that jeopardizes national security, public safety, and social order."

The *Wall Street Journal* of 11 October 2017[41] reported that the Chinese state has asked each of Tencent, Baidu and Alibaba to offer it a stake in their companies and a direct role in corporate decisions. Some observers might take the view that such steps are unnecessary in China in order to secure state (and CPC) influence, but apparently they are. There can be little doubt that the Chinese leadership sees social networks and platforms that open up freedom of expression unavailable through other media as difficult to control. Not the least because Chinese citizens are avid users of such networks. The main point for the state and the CPC is that if this continues unchecked the three companies will have a deeper insight into citizens and be able to exercise a stronger control over them than the state/CPC.

China, the United States and Europe all confront the same dilemma. It is sometimes seen as a question of freedom of expression, but it has little to do with free speech as this is normally perceived. The question is, who decides what goes on the net.

China has witnessed with pride the growth of these companies and has hitherto regarded them as cornerstones for turning the country into a high-tech nation. Now the matter of who is in control has suddenly become a question. Increasingly, the big data companies have assumed the power to control what people and companies communicate over the networks and over the infrastructure serving to facilitate this communication. This is a power outside of national governments that has never been seen before. And as the companies operate globally, this power game cannot be confined to the national level. The attitude chosen will to a large degree determine the role the companies play globally. Who will win the battle to influence the mindset of the billions of people not living in China, the United States and Europe? To what extent will these other nation-states be dragged into conflict among the data companies when one nation asks for help in confronting the government of another one? The US government has already intervened in a case against Apple that was brought before the European Court of Justice.[42]

Behind the curtain lurks the prospect of extraterritorial jurisdiction by a limited number of the major powers. This has been seen over a number of years, with the United States beginning the Proliferation Security Initiative, where they would stop foreign-flagged ships in international waters in order to search for weapons of mass destruction. The wish to either contain or to use the big data companies may open the door for similar activities in the future.

The situation of data companies versus the state reflects a political power game: Who is in control? Who decides? The other side to the coin are the questions of how to run the economy, how to determine the growth rate and to decide what "growth" actually is, and how is the increased wealth to be distributed.

The Coming Power Game: Economic Model; Sustainability

The country or society that is able to catch the global mood and to sketch out a working model that combines ethics and economics will become the alpha male of globalization.

The United States has occupied that position for the last seventy-five years, and it still holds cards to play. But over the last ten to twenty years America has gradually abandoned the values it had formerly defended with vigour, conviction and strength leaving doubt as to what America stands for. Question marks as to whether international institutions (the WTO, IMF and World Bank) are actually serving US interests leaves doubt over its role as an upholder of institutionalized economic globalization. The steps it has taken lately reveal that the United States no longer sees eye to eye with a large number of its allies, partners or other countries on fundamental issues for the societal model of the future.

The issue of sustainability goes far beyond environmental quality and global warming. It is indeed a question of which societal model a country will choose to adopt. With an increasing global population, combined with rising income per capita, it is inevitable that this will take over as the dominant policy question.

The United States does not fully grasp the significance of the need to take a long-term perspective in managing scarce resources. China and Europe in contrast seem to have done so. Perhaps the explanation is that the United States is a relatively new nation-state and has not met the challenge of the kind of existential crises, for example natural catastrophes, that have harassed China and Europe, driving home the message that there are limits to how much nature can deliver. The American attitude, going back to the nineteenth century of "going West", reflects a mentality of plenty—that you just need to look for it.

China has put forward a long and impressive list of national targets, and it also subscribes to a global target. There is no need to list all the figures, plans and achievements. It suffices to recall the July 2017 report by CNN[43] that "China's National Energy Administration in January established a mandatory target to reduce coal energy consumption. It also set a goal for clean energy to meet 20% of China's energy needs by 2030. Analysts expect China to easily meet that target. Greenpeace noted in a report[44] that the country's clean energy consumption rose to 12% at the end of 2015."

This massive reorientation of policy took place in response to pressure from below. The Chinese population is not willing to live with a deteriorating environment as the companion of economic growth. Both traditional media and social networks have been reporting the human costs. The Chinese people have reacted and demanded that the CPC redraws its policy; aware of the need to legitimize its hold on power, the CPC has responded.

Doubts persist as to whether China has the financial clout and technological know-how to carry this policy shift through. It has the financial clout, certainly. But it is not likely that it possesses the technological know-how yet. To address this the government has launched a colossal investment programme in R&D, innovation and technology. China spends (2016 figures) 2.1 per cent of its GDP on R&D.[45] In 2006, the target set for R&D spend by 2020 was 2.5 per cent of GDP.[46] President Xi Jinping's speech to the Nineteenth Party Congress left no doubt that this course will be pursued: "We will strengthen basic research in applied sciences, launch major national science and technology projects and prioritize innovation in key technologies."[47]

But is China willing and able to share technological knowledge with other countries? The political leadership may see the benefits of doing so, but it will need to convince the population. Will the Chinese people be willing to offer knowledge they have paid for to other countries? If the answer is no, China will be seen as an egocentric power, or maybe even an egoistic one. If the answer is yes, China will be perceived as a benevolent power that uses its clout not just for its own interests but with a global perspective. The litmus test to come is whether the Chinese population will gradually turn its feelings of nationalism, from pride in what the country has achieved, into a sense that it is worthwhile to spread the model to other countries, even if this means sacrificing economic advantages for China.

Foreign policy nowadays is pursued through social networks, in trying to shape perceptions and to rally people around the globe to support the same objective, irrespective of where they live. The fact the United States left the Paris Agreement on global warming does not mean that US society or businesses agreed with the move.[48]

China has an opportunity to forge a majority—in particular, a majority of people in "recalcitrant" nation-states—offering them leadership in value-based policies. It has the chance to assume global leadership in one of the most important—perhaps *the* most important—soft foreign policy issues of the coming decades: sustainability. Never mind the governments.

It looks like the United States and a number of other nation-states are isolating themselves from what may be called the mainstream group.

The European Union may be a larger and more important player than China. In 2015 the European Commission put forward a comprehensive action plan called "Closing the Loop, An EU action plan for the circular economy". This plan highlights product lifecycles and seeks greater recycling and re-use, bringing benefits for both the environment and the economy. The plans aims to extract the maximum value and use from all raw materials, products and waste, fostering energy savings and reducing greenhouse gas emissions. The proposals cover the full lifecycle of products: from production and consumption to waste management and the market for secondary raw materials.[49] In 2019 the European Commission reported that the fifty-four planned actions had been implemented with success. It pointed out that not only had the qualitative ambitions—improving the environment—been achieved, but tangible business opportunities had arisen, resulting in economic growth.[50]

On 4 March 2019, the European Commission adopted a comprehensive report on the implementation of the Circular Economy Action Plan. The report presents the main achievements under the action plan, sketches out the future challenges that will shape the economy, and paves the way towards a climate-neutral, circular economy, where pressures on natural and freshwater resources and ecosystems are minimized. It is a follow up to a plan launched in 2015, which is progressing according to schedule. It aims at recycling rates of 65 per cent for municipal waste by 2035 and 70 per cent of packaging material by 2030.[51]

Compared with the strong deregulation in the United States initiated by the Trump administration—rolling back a large number of regulations implemented during the Obama administration aimed at reducing pollution—it is not impossible that Europe and China will forge some mutual understanding on the vital point of tackling the question of the ecosphere, and move towards a model with a higher priority on the quality of life, ultimately coming closer to 100 per cent recycling. If this was to happen, it would be an example of values shaping alliances, which could spread to other items on the global agenda, shifting the global power structure significantly.

As to whether China "will make it" is uncertain. There is no doubt about the political determination, and the money is there. It is possible that a strong partnership between China and the EU will emerge in an effort to solve pollution problems on the basis of high recycling. If so, some US states could be drawn into this group, as also may be the case for several Asian nations.

China Wants Access to the World Economy

In the course of 2017, President Xi Jinping made it abundantly clear that China supports globalization and is open to the world.[52] China has reached the stage in its economic development where economic growth will never again reach the heights it has seen in recent decades. Nonetheless, achieving high growth and remaining fully integrated in the global economy are imperative.

The backpedalling by the United States and Britain poses a problem. Can China count on the existing system to serve as a platform for its further integration. Perhaps; but, perhaps not. Seen through the prism of Chinese politics, this is not reassuring, with it forcing China to build its own access to economic globalization.

In terms of foreign and security policy, there are fears that in the event of a conflict the US Navy may cut China off, or at least make it difficult and costly for it to maintain its integration with the global economy. The mere fact of such threats will pose a policy dilemma for China.

For the time being there is no substitute for the existing system. China is busy however building a political and technical infrastructure that is providing it access to other countries. This has so far been on a regional basis.

The Regional Comprehensive Economic Partnership (RCEP) is offered as a platform for regional free trade, which is to a certain degree compensating for the TPP after the American withdrawal.

The Belt and Road Initiative (BRI) is a very ambitious project, both financially and politically. It aims at securing a transport infrastructure for China with a large group of countries in Asia (Southeast Asia, South Asia, the Middle East, Iran, Central Asia and Europe).

The Asian Infrastructure Investment Bank (AIIB) is presented as some kind of World Bank and Asian Development Bank (ADB) plus, but it serves in reality as the financial arm of China's policy to keep the door open to the global economy. It can and certainly will finance many projects under the BRI label. As long as the existing system functions, AIIB supplements it. Should hiccups occur, it can stand in for, and will eventually replace, global financial institutions. In the meantime it provides China with experience of how to run an international bank.

Seen from the Chinese perspective, it is a win-win proposition. A large political and logistic structure is being built on a regional basis, where China is naturally primus inter pares, and without confronting the existing global system. Eventually it may be integrated into the global system, whether or not it will be reformed in some way, without much fuss. Should the global system begin to crack, these initiatives can be turned into global structures, replacing or supplementing the post-World War II system.

In a similar fashion, China is using its foreign aid strategically. By far the two largest recipients are Russia and Pakistan.[53] A quick glance at the map explains why. Russia controls the land route to Europe. Pakistan controls access to the Indian Ocean.

The Transition to Multinational Companies

The attitudes of the United States and Britain to globalization reflect the power shift that has seen the waning of US power, China as a rising power, and the emergence of a large number of middle-sized powers. There has been a revolt against the United States pursuing its superpower behaviour, whereby it can do whatever it wants to do and other countries can only do what it allows them to do.

At stake is whether globalization will continue or whether slogans such as "America first" and "take back control" augur a more national and less international global model. If, as is most likely, globalization continues, the next question is whether it will be institutionalized as the post–World War II system, and what kind of international law will emerge.

For China's political leaders, these are questions that must be addressed. So far China has let it be known that it wants globalization and an open world, but these pledges are thin on substance. The only potential partner to build an institutionalized and rules-based global system is Europe, with it sharing with China many worries and policy ambitions. Still, there are obstacles to China and Europe coming closer together. Continental Europe has, since 1945, looked to the United States. The exit by Britain from the EU could be a harbinger of fundamental differences in the societal model between continental Europe and the United States/Britain. At the same time, it draws attention to the congruous elements between the European and Chinese societal models. It is a hard nut though to crack for Europe to deviate from the United States, even with Donald Trump as president.

Two issues however are pushing Europe in that direction:

1. The rise of the big data companies and the potential power game between these companies and the state. Continental Europe and China have so far adopted similar attitudes (in trying to control these companies). The United States and Britain look more likely to try to merge the state with these companies.
2. Sustainability, with continental Europe and China favouring a common approach anchored on a forceful attempt to reduce pollution and global warming—indeed moving towards a societal model aimed eventually at a waste-neutral economic model.

The Chinese and the Europeans might begin to look at these possibilities, but they cannot forge a new global model without the consent or, even better, the support of a number of other countries. The rest of the world will watch closely in order to join the winner.

Even more important is the fact that the flywheel for such a partnership is people power. It is the people—clearly so in Europe and perhaps it is also becoming that way in China—who demand protection from the big data companies and insist that multinationals pay taxes. It is also the people who are driving thinking about the circular economy.

The Americans have understood and applied a basic theorem of global leadership: The willingness to sacrifice their own interests in order to achieve a global solution. This is a hard sell at home, but the United States has managed to do this for more than sixty years.

Unless the Chinese and the Europeans can and will do the same, they will falter. If so, multinational companies may enter the arena of the global power play and outshine the nation-states. The nation-states and institutionalized economic globalization may still be visible, but the real power play will be fought among multinationals and between multinationals, nation-states and global institutions.

Key Points

The global steering system has become unpredictable. This is bad news for China, which was looking forward to reaping the benefits of the system it joined thirty-five years ago. The abdication by the United States and Britain as leaders offers China the opportunity to shape a new system without breaking up the existing one—evolution, not revolution. This is taking place at the same time as ICTs and social networks have introduced a new power game around the shaping of perceptions: from that of nation-state versus nation-state to the colossal data companies versus the state. Data companies have greater insights into the behaviour of people and businesses than the states do, and they use this knowledge to influence and to ultimately control behavioural patterns. Three of these companies are in China: Baidu, Alibaba, and Tencent. A number of indicators point to common interests between China and Continental Europe: their attitudes towards the data companies, on maintaining an open global system, sustainability, and awareness of social external diseconomies. Initiatives on the part of China such as the BRI, AIIB and RCEP illustrate an embryonic move to frame a future global system without disrupting the existing one.

The starting point for this dismantling of the existing system was the global financial crisis of 2008–9, which unmasked the weakness of the nation-state—in particular, the United States and Britain—while at the same time giving a clear signal of the robustness of the Chinese economy.

Notes

1. This chapter is an updated and amended version of my chapter, "Global Governance: How Asia Shapes the World", in *Handbook on China and Globalization*, edited by Huiyao Wang and Liu Miao (Cheltenham: Elgar, 2019).
2. https://en.wikipedia.org/wiki/German_Americans.
3. "The mountains are high and the emperor is far away" is a Chinese proverb dating back to the Yuan Dynasty that is often used to explain how difficult it is for the central government to make the provinces toe the line.
4. https://www.goodreads.com/quotes/84250-anti-intellectualism-has-been-a-constant-thread-winding-its-way-through.
5. https://www.reuters.com/article/us-autos-emissions-california/california-sues-u-s-agencies-over-data-on-vehicle-emissions-freeze-idUSKCN1RH2G4.
6. Italics mine.
7. https://www.bloomberg.com/news/articles/2017-01-08/china-s-pyrrhic-growth-victory-spurs-2017-shift-to-contain-risks.
8. Carl von Clausewitz, *On War*, edited and translated by Michael Howard and Bernhard Brodie (Princeton, NJ: Princeton University Press [1832] 1976).
9. Graham Allison, *Destined for War: Can America and China Escape Thucydides's Trap?* (Boston: Houghton Mifflin Harcourt, 2017).
10. https://www.usatoday.com/story/money/markets/2017/05/03/wall-street-earnings/101168864/.
11. http://www.macworld.co.uk/feature/apple/where-are-apple-products-made-3633832/.
12. Norman Angell, *The Great Illusion* (Kindle ed.) (The Floating Press, [1910] 2013).
13. Joergen Oerstroem Moeller, "China's Effort to Redefine Corporate Governance", *World Future Review* (Fall 2012): 5–11.
14. https://www.nytimes.com/2017/10/18/world/asia/china-xi-jinping-party-congress.html.
15. Jonathan Woetzel, "From Third World to First Class", *Milken Institute Review* (2Q 2019): 22–34.
16. https://www.bloomberg.com/opinion/articles/2019-04-07/cic-investments-have-gone-low-profile-a-new-chairman-won-t-help.
17. http://www.economist.com/node/13527969.
18. http://www.oecd.org/daf/anti-bribery/oecdantibriberyconvention.htm.
19. Jonas Parello-Plesner and Mathieu Duchâtel, *China's Strong Arm: Protecting Citizens and Assets Abroad* (London: IISS, 2015).
20. http://www.abc.net.au/news/2016-12-09/s-kidman-and-co-sale-to-rinehart-approved/8106694.

21. http://www.reuters.com/article/us-nexen-cnooc/cnooc-closes-15-1-billion-acquisition-of-canadas-nexen-idUSBRE91O1A420130225.
22. https://www.whitehouse.gov/the-press-office/2017/09/13/statement-press-secretary-president-donald-j-trumps-decision-regarding.
23. Joergen Oerstroem Moeller, "China's Investments in Europe: Lessons for South East Asia", *ISEAS Perspectives*, no. 2017/56, 24 July 2017.
24. https://www.bloomberg.com/news/articles/2017-05-10/china-s-246-billion-takeover-spree-is-crumbling-as-sellers-balk.
25. http://variety.com/2017/biz/asia/china-spells-out-overseas-deals-restrictions-1202532479/.
26. https://www.cnbc.com/2017/06/16/chinas-real-estate-investors-on-a-200b-global-spending-spree.html.
27. https://www.forbes.com/sites/grantfeller/2016/06/14/this-is-the-real-reason-microsoft-bought-linkedin/#64362ef9f04a.
28. Interview with Knowledge@Wharton, 13 October 2017. http://knowledge.wharton.upenn.edu/article/world-without-mind/?utm_source=kw_newsletter&utm_medium=email&utm_campaign=2017-10-19.
29. https://www.wired.com/2016/05/facebook-microsoft-laying-giant-cable-across-atlantic/, http://money.cnn.com/2016/10/13/technology/facebook-google-undersea-cable-china-pacific/index.html, http://www.wired.co.uk/article/google-facebook-plcn-internet-cable.
30. https://yourstory.com/2017/05/apple-q2-2017/ plus http://www.telegraph.co.uk/finance/11038180/Global-firms-sitting-on-7-trillion-war-chest.html plus https://www.economist.com/news/business-and-finance/21722809-their-excuses-doing-so-dont-add-up-tech-firms-hoard-huge-cash-piles.
31. http://stats.oecd.org/Index.aspx?DataSetCode=GERD_FUNDS.
32. http://www.businessinsider.sg/apple-rd-spend-charts-2017-2/?r=US&IR=T.
33. https://www.ft.com/content/d5397a08-4667-11e7-8d27-59b4dd6296b8.
34. http://financials.morningstar.com/ratios/r.html?t=TCEHY.
35. http://financials.morningstar.com/ratios/r.html?t=BABA.
36. https://www.theverge.com/2013/6/6/4403868/nsa-fbi-mine-data-apple-google-facebook-microsoft-others-prism; https://www.washingtonpost.com/investigations/us-intelligence-mining-data-from-nine-us-internet-companies-in-broad-secret-program/2013/06/06/3a0c0da8-cebf-11e2-8845-d970ccb04497_story.html?hpid=z1&utm_term=.7abdd012a930.
37. http://ec.europa.eu/newsroom/just/item-detail.cfm?item_id=605819.
38. http://ec.europa.eu/justice/data-protection/reform/files/regulation_oj_en.pdf.
39. http://europa.eu/rapid/press-release_IP-17-3702_en.htm.
40. https://thediplomat.com/2017/09/china-fines-its-top-3-internet-giants-for-violating-cybersecurity-law/.

41. https://www.wsj.com/articles/beijing-pushes-for-a-direct-hand-in-chinas-big-tech-firms-1507758314.
42. http://thehill.com/policy/technology/340667-report-us-supporting-apples-appeal-of-eu-tax-case.
43. http://money.cnn.com/2017/07/18/technology/china-us-clean-energy-solar-farm/index.html.
44. http://www.greenpeace.org/eastasia/press/releases/climate-energy/2017/By-2030-Chinas-wind-and-solar-industry-could-replace-fossil-energy-sources-to-the-tune-of-300-million-tonnes-of-standard-coal-per-year/.
45. http://www.chinadaily.com.cn/china/2017-10/19/content_33459635.htm.
46. http://www.gov.cn/english/2006-02/09/content_183426.htm.
47. https://www.washingtonpost.com/business/technology/chinas-xi-calls-for-more-technology-development/2017/10/18/bd46d1be-b3c4-11e7-9b93-b97043e57a22_story.html?utm_term=.98f4876f0018.
48. Joergen Oerstroem Moeller, "Values Inspire Foreign-Policy Revolution across Borders", *YaleGlobal online,* 22 August 2017.
49. https://eur-lex.europa.eu/legal-content/EN/TXT/?uri=CELEX:52015DC0614.
50. https://ec.europa.eu/commission/news/commission-delivers-circular-economy-action-plan-2019-mar-04_en.
51. http://ec.europa.eu/environment/circular-economy/index_en.htm.
52. "We should commit ourselves to growing an open global economy", speech at World Economic Forum, Davos, 17 January 2007, CGTN, https://america.cgtn.com/2017/01/17/full-text-of-xi-jinping-keynote-at-the-world-economic-forum; "China will not close its door to the world; it will only become more and more open", highlights of Xi's report to the Nineteenth Party Congress, *Global Times,* 18 October 2107, http://www.globaltimes.cn/content/1070853.shtml.
53. http://www.scmp.com/news/china/diplomacy-defence/article/2114881/china-course-overtake-us-worlds-biggest-foreign-aid.

5

Significance of the Global Financial Crisis

The global financial crisis of 2008–9 morphed into political, economic and social problems, mainly for the United States, demonstrating its fading power within the global picture. Domestic disruptions and dislocations of a magnitude few had foreseen followed. It disclosed how fragile the US political system had become, confronting it with events that required bipartisan measures to address in the interests of the nation and, even more so, in the interests of the world.

History may well record the crisis as an event that changed the attitudes of Americans. In 2011, 38 per cent of Americans were of the opinion that the United States stood above all other countries in the world. In 2017, the figure was 29 per cent. Even if the percentage of Americans saying that there are other countries that are better than the United States has not gone above 15 per cent, the smaller percentage that see their country as the best is significant, as it signifies a reduced willingness to finance and support a policy of "exporting" the model. The support for the kind of foreign and security policies that the United States had for decades sustained—policies anchored in values—is now much weaker.[1]

A survey conducted in twenty-two countries in 2011 revealed that 66 per cent of people had a favourable view of the United States, compared to 25 per cent who saw it as a major threat. Only five years later, the figure for those with a favourable view of the United States was down to 51 per cent, with those seeing it as a threat having risen to 45 per cent. The biggest swing was seen in Germany (30 percentage points), France (29 percentage points) and Mexico (26 percentage points). The figure for the other neighbour of the United States, Canada, was at 23 per cent.[2]

These two surveys convey the picture of a superpower that is losing both domestic and international support for its global role—especially from its allies and neighbouring countries. The figures for its two neighbours augur fundamental trouble, with 66 per cent of Mexicans and 46 per cent of Canadians saying that the United States is a major threat. With regard to US policy and its position in Asia, the percentage of people classifying the United States as a major threat among its two main allies, Japan and Korea, are 66 and 67 per cent, respectively. This result can hardly be seen as a propitious climate for shaping an Asian policy; or, to be more direct, a policy vis-à-vis China with support from allies in the region.

This attrition of values is happening at the same time as the US share of global GDP has gone into a nosedive. In reality, there is nothing surprising in this, as history recounts that no power can account indefinitely for more than a third of global GDP. For the United States, it has fallen from an estimated 50 per cent at the end of World War II to 38 per cent by 1970, and to 22 per cent in 2018.

The combination of soft power (values) and hard power (military) depends on economic strength to finance an active international policy. Soft power can only be effective if the use of hard power is seen by both opponents and allies as credible should soft power fail. A lower share of global GDP indicates that the United States is not capable of financing a war, making the threat of hard power to back up its soft power less convincing.

Economic strength provides the means to build and maintain a large and effective military force. Over the decades, the number of ships, aircraft and combat divisions has fallen, partly because money is no longer flowing as lavishly as it used to. Allies no longer benefit from US financial assistance, or at least not to the extent they had in the past.

The use of money as an effective instrument of soft power is difficult. Since 1945, money has been one of the arrows in the quiver used to convince countries all over the world that it might be better to follow the advice given by the United States.

The benefits for a country of participating in economic globalization can be said to be broadly proportional to its share of global GDP. The higher its share, the more it exports, leading to an improvement in living standards. And, more importantly, it becomes a trade and investment partner for other countries. With its share for many decades after the end of World War II above 30 per cent, the United States reaped a large benefit that directly and indirectly justified a commitment to not only support the system but to also take the lead. Numerous global negotiating rounds ended with a positive outcome because the United States at the end of the day was willing to forego some advantages for itself in the interests of a global agreement. This policy reflected to a degree a moral stance inside the American establishment. But it also reflected the basic fact that the business sector—and most people, for that matter—saw the long-term economic advantage for the United States of doing so. In 2018, the share for the United States was 22 per cent, which signals reduced benefits for it flowing from economic globalization. The equation of benefits versus costs/commitments has turned from positive to negative.

The financial crisis forced on the United States represented the acceleration of a process that had already been visible following the invasion of Iraq in 2003 and that had become deeper during the Obama administration. This gave witness to a realigning of costs and commitments of the US global role, with a commensurate effect on the benefits. As the benefits could not be augmented in light of the share of GDP falling, and with no prospect of raising it, the only thing to do was to lower costs and commitments. This is tantamount to a strategic withdrawal.

The realignment has become a cornerstone of the Trump administration, albeit one masked by a robust vocabulary that some observers would label boisterous. NATO allies have been told that the United States might not necessarily act in accordance with article five of the treaty (an attack against one ally is considered an attack against all allies). And the United States has been manoeuvring vis-à-vis North Korea without even informing, even less consulting, its two main Asian allies Japan and South Korea.

In reality the United States is heavily in debt, with public debt of close to US$22 trillion. If intragovernmental debt (debt owed by the federal government to federal agencies) is subtracted from this, the outstanding debt is about US$16 trillion, which is close to 85 per cent of the country's GDP. A total of 40 per cent of the treasuries marked to finance this debt—mainly in the form of ten-year treasury bonds—are held by foreign investors and governments. The rest are held by US banks, pension funds, etc. China and Japan each hold around US$1.2 trillion, representing a little more than 6 per cent of the treasury bonds issued.[3] This situation has arisen because since the 1970s the federal government has only been in surplus during four years—1998, 1999, 2000 and 2001. And since 1975 the US balance of goods and services (current account) with other countries has been negative. There is no way around the conclusion that the United States is living beyond its means and is borrowing to finance activities for which its citizens will not pay. US politicians are not prepared to tell the country's citizens that the situation is untenable. In the terminology of economics, the United States is running a savings deficit, and encroaching on the willingness of other countries to allow it to do so. The equation did not pose much of a problem whilst the United States was the leading nation in globalization. Now, however, it is lurking just around the corner as a major problem.

The debt has to be serviced, and there are two ways this can be done. First, the issued treasury bonds are mostly for five or ten years. When they mature, the debt incurred has to be paid in full. It can be calculated that the average expiry time of outstanding US treasury bonds is 64.5 months,[4] which means that in a little over six years the bulk of treasury bonds will have been renewed with new bonds replacing the bonds that have matured and been paid back—even with no change in the total debt. The United States is in the uncomfortable position of having to burden the capital markets every year just to renew its borrowings.

As the federal government is still in deficit, and with this debt increasing, borrowing goes up by more treasury bonds being issued. The amount of outstanding treasury bonds increases every year, crowding out other kinds of borrowing on the capital market—for example, by the business sector—and sowing anxiety about whether the United States will still be able to pay it back. Obviously, the larger the amount to be paid back, the more creditors will worry; and the more they worry, the less willing they will be to buy new treasury bonds.

No one knows when this borrowing will run into a roadblock. So far the United States has been able to capitalize not only on its global role but also on the lack of alternatives. But it would be risky to count on such a benevolent situation lasting forever.

The United States has to pay interest to the creditors buying treasury bonds. The net interest burden is currently 9.8 per cent of the federal budget, which translates into 1.3 per cent of GDP. Projections point to a figure of 19 per cent of the federal budget, equal to 3.1 per cent of GDP, by 2028.[5] These projections assume fairly good economic growth and a favourable interest rate. These assumptions may turn out to be realistic, but the risk is on the downside in the sense that lower growth and/or higher interest rates will aggravate the net interest burden as a share of both the federal budget and GDP. Gradually, the net interest burden will eat up other lines of the federal budget. The debt is financed over the federal budget's discretionary spending, accounting for about 23 per cent of the total budget (US$4.1 trillion). Projections show that in 2023 the net interest burden will exceed defence spending and that in 2025 it will be the biggest item on the federal budget, rising from US$389 billion in 2019 to US$914 billion by 2028.[6]

Whichever way you look at it, it is a festering sore that is swallowing money that could have been spent on boosting the economy, promoting technology or improving social coherence. It is difficult to see how the United States will solve this problem, which is threatening its political and social stability and the funding of its military. The money has to be found somewhere. A tax increase would be the conventional response, but this seems to be politically blocked. And to do so would have the disadvantage of slowing the economy. Diverting money from other budget lines is becoming increasingly difficult as close to two thirds of the budget is mandatory spending, leaving only US$1.4 trillion available from which to find the money.

The American capital market has for decades been both the biggest and most efficient one, without any real competitor. This may seem rather paradoxical in light of the United States now having grown into the largest net debtor in the world. There are several reasons however that explain this phenomenon. A well-functioning capital market is a natural companion for the largest economy in the world, irrespective of its performance. This strong position was built in the ten to fifteen years following World War II, when there was no other competitor, as the British economy was suffering and at the same time its empire was being dismantled.

There are huge advantages to being the largest and, in the eyes of many, the best capital market in the world. The rest of the world, in particular countries with a savings surplus, do not have a capital market or financial institutions in which to invest their money. They deposit their savings with American financial institutions, which take over the role of shuffling not only American savings but also the savings of other countries around the world. There is no doubt, at least up until the global financial crisis, that these institutions did this with vigilance and they took care of the interests of their customers. But a lack of competition made them commit hubris, and increasingly led them to look at making money for themselves. In 2012 a former Goldman Sachs executive wrote in the *New York Times* that he resigned because the company had become toxic and destructive.[7]

With this attitude the US financial institutions earned colossal profits, which contributed handsomely to exports of services and helped to reduce the deficit in the balance of payments. Furthermore, the US financial institutions, whether deliberately or not, invested with an eye to America's interests because that is what they had learned and what they found natural. It was also about such assets that they knew best. Indirectly, this enhanced US soft power as the United States was in a position to invest more abroad, actually much more, than its own economy would have permitted.

On top of this, the United States had a near monopoly of rating agencies. Countries around the world were dependent on what US economists raised and trained in American universities thought about their economy. If the verdict was negative, capital markets reacted by not buying their bonds, with the result that costs for borrowing went up. If it was positive, borrowing was plain sailing. Again, deliberately or not, this was done with an American perspective as the economists were trained to think like Americans. They often forgot to include social and local conditions in their prescriptions, assuming that what would work in the United States would also work in a developing country. Two of the three major ratings agencies—Standard & Poors and Moody's—are based in the United States, while the third—Fitch—has dual headquarters in New York and London.

One wonders how it could be the case, but none of these agencies saw the global financial crisis coming, despite all their expertise (or, rather, apparent expertise) under their roofs. The dismal record of the rating agencies did not affect them, and they are still dominating the game and enhancing US soft power in the financial sector.

However, competition is emerging. China is setting up rating agencies. Four currently exist, with some of them linked to one of the big American rating agencies. Judged by performance, until now they have found it difficult to strike the right balance, as their rating of companies issuing bonds on the Chinese capital market—the third biggest in the world—has not proved to be very good.[8]

Should the US debt explode, it might well have a spillover effect on the American rating agencies, all of whom still rate the United States very positively, with Fitch giving it AAA, Standard & Poors AA+ and Moody's Aaa. None of them apparently see any major problems ahead, despite the figures unequivocally auguring a future crisis.

The US dollar is still the global reserve currency. Neither the euro nor any of the Asian currencies, including the yen and renminbi (which, by the way, is not convertible), have succeeded in making a major dent in its preponderance.

However, the US dollar reigns on borrowed time. The reserve currency has historically followed the strongest economy. First it was Britain's pound sterling, and then it was the US dollar. Currency reserves are held to eventually buy goods and services abroad and to fund foreign direct investments. This explains why the global reserve currency follows the largest economy. This is where foreign countries want to buy, to where they want to sell, and where they want to invest in the business sector.

If the projections that say the Chinese economy will continue to grow at a much faster rate than that of the United States prove to be correct—and this is likely—sooner or later the reserve currency sceptre will pass to the renminbi. There will be a long-time lag as international investors and countries take time to make the swap, and so far the gap between the economies does not warrant it. The comparison between the two economies depends on the use of official currency rates (the United States wins) or purchasing power parity (PPP) (China wins). But China's GDP per capita, even with a PPP calculation, is only about a third that of the United States. This means we can safely conclude the renminbi will not replace the US dollar for a couple of decades.

That is not the same as saying the US dollar will not face attacks and be forced to give ground on some fronts. The oil trade is especially vulnerable. Saudi Arabia has on at least two occasions contemplated switching to another unit of account.[9] In 2017 this was instigated by China for oil trade. But such changes, should they come, would be classified as peripheral and as not touching the global position of the US dollar.

The dollar looks safe for now. But, as with the financial institutions, should the country's debt explode it will probably undermine the role of the US dollar. The consequences will be the same. US soft power through global finance will be decimated.

Key Points

The global financial crisis signalled that the US economy is no longer strong enough to underpin the role of uncontested global super power. The economic decline was followed by an erosion of US moral authority both at home and abroad.

The Trump administration has acted vigorously to realign benefits and the costs/commitments of US engagement on the global stage, and the only way it has been able to do this is through a strategic withdrawal by reducing costs and commitments. This has alienated its allies and led to the dismantling of the global steering system—but a strategic withdrawal connotes that the United States no longer needs allies or a global system.

The message is that the era of the United States as the flywheel of the global economy has come to an end. A new global economy will be shaped by demographics, technology and energy.

Notes

1. https://www.pewresearch.org/fact-tank/2017/06/30/most-americans-say-the-u-s-is-among-the-greatest-countries-in-the-world/.
2. https://www.pewresearch.org/fact-tank/2019/02/14/more-people-around-the-world-see-u-s-power-and-influence-as-a-major-threat-to-their-country/.

3. https://www.thebalance.com/who-owns-the-u-s-national-debt-3306124 and Congressional Budget Office (CBO).
4. https://www.quora.com/What-is-the-average-maturity-date-on-U-S-debt
5. CBO data.
6. https://www.pgpf.org/blog/2018/11/we-will-soon-be-spending-more-on-national-debt-interest-than-on-these-vital-programs.
7. https://www.nytimes.com/2012/03/14/opinion/why-i-am-leaving-goldman-sachs.html.
8. https://www.ft.com/content/e6ea3c7c-55f8-11e9-91f9-b6515a54c5b1.
9. https://www.cnbc.com/2017/10/11/china-will-compel-saudi-arabia-to-trade-oil-in-yuan--and-thats-going-to-affect-the-us-dollar.html; https://www.reuters.com/article/us-saudi-usa-oil-exclusive/exclusive-saudi-arabia-threatens-to-ditch-dollar-oil-trades-to-stop-nopec-sources-idUSKCN1RH008.

6

Global Economics Horizon 2035

The first phase of economic globalization in modern times lasted from the early 1950s to the first decade of the twenty-first century. It was shaped by national economies adapting to a global market and was dominated by the liberalization of trade and investments. The impulse for this came from the transformation of national economies that spread growth to other countries, drawing them into globalization. To make it work, rules-based international organizations were set up. Some nation-states went further and established a system of economic integration, such as the European Union (EU)—both an economic and a political enterprise—and the Association of Southeast Asian Nations (ASEAN).

The sinews of the global economy over the next fifteen years will be neither the national economies nor the conventional well-known forces such as trade and investment, but rather demographics, technology and energy, and how these will interact with each other. They will frame the conditions for the national economies to thrive; those that cannot do so will face a lacklustre economic situation. The impulse will be in the opposite direction to what it was in the first phase. This time it will be from internationalization to the national economies.

The political problem will be how to exploit the opportunities that this interaction will put on the table, and the question of where nation-states will be willing to take further steps to globalize their economies despite the short-term problems of restructuring.

Demographics[1]

The size of the labour force (the share of the population aged 15–64 years of age) and the dependency ratio (the share of those aged over 65) are decisive parameters in attempts to forecast the future economic global competitiveness of a nation-state.

For many years the Chinese labour force knew only one direction—it was going up. When Deng Xiaoping initiated reforms in the late 1970s, he gambled on cheap labour costs combined with a reasonably skilled labour force, discipline and willingness, plus the ability to work hard. It turned out to be a colossal success. China became the centre for manufacturing, and it crowded out the industrialized countries as well as competitors among emerging markets and developing economies, coming close to monopolizing labour-intensive, low-cost manufacturing.

But nothing lasts for ever. As the figures in Table 6.1 show, the labour force is falling. The last year that it was still going up was 2015. From a peak of about 1,025 million, the labour force will have fallen to 825 million by 2050, and will continue downwards to reach 615 million by 2100.

Labour costs are going up in China, with this core sector of the economy losing steam. The consequence is that labour-intensive, low-cost manufacturing is migrating to other countries. Some of it is going to Southeast Asian nation-states such as Vietnam, the Philippines, Indonesia and Myanmar.

The long-term destination in a horizon 2050 analysis is South Asia, primarily India, with a labour force projected to rise almost 40 per cent from year 2000 to 2050. Pakistan and Bangladesh may claim a share of this, but the large part will go to India. This is, however, not without its problems. India has the labour force, but it lacks the infrastructure to link manufacturing plants across the country and ship the goods to the final consumers, many of whom will be overseas. Ports, railways

TABLE 6.1
Population Aged 15–65 Years (millions)

Country/Year	1950	2000	2025	2050	2100
China	332	1,025	1,000	825	615
India	223	800	1,000	1,100	931

and roads need to be built. Furthermore, the labour force has not been trained to do this job. Most of the workers are without basic skills, requiring a strong effort to train and educate people.

All this requires money, which India does not have. The government's finances are not bad, with government debt at about two thirds of GDP and a budget deficit of 3.4 per cent of GDP. The balance of payments (current account) shows a deficit of 1.7 per cent of GDP.[2] The country's federal structure may create obstacles for infrastructure investments. It is therefore likely that India will need some help from outside to perform the required economic miracle, and the most likely country to assist will be China. China's savings surplus is disappearing, but it is still financially strong enough to invest abroad. India has a savings deficit. The total amount needed to update the infrastructure has been estimated at US$770 billion, with a programme for 2018–19 of US$92 billion.[3] China knows from experience what training and education will be required to prepare the work force for labour-intensive, low-cost manufacturing.

It will be one of the biggest—perhaps the biggest—international economic restructuring the world has ever seen. The advantage for China is that the migration of this economic sector is going to take place anyway, as China is pricing itself out of the market, so it would be better for it to try to keep some of the benefits by participating in building plants in another country. It will be a good investment for China. Chinese investments in India are already fairly substantial and have been rising fast. The estimated amount of investment is US$11–12 billion, with more than seven hundred Chinese companies involved.[4]

The advantage for India is that the difficulties of doing it alone without outside assistance speak for themselves. Neither the money nor the expertise may be there. It would be the rational move to link up with China, even if political feelings may stand in the way. And yet, research[5] has shown that between 2015 and 2017, media sentiment towards Chinese investment in Indian infrastructure has been turning more positive.

Whether China and India will be able to cooperate on this gigantic transformation may well decide the future of economic globalization. If it goes ahead, the omens are that for at least the next ten to twenty years economic globalization will be supported by strong growth and a good climate between these two Asian powers, with a combined population of around 2.5 billion people and linking what will be the world's second-largest economy (or the largest, depending on the method of calculation) with the fifth-largest, creating an enormous power house. If it does not go ahead, both countries will be caught wrong footed, losing steam in their drive for economic growth and competitiveness, with dire social and political consequences as the millions of people who are not able to find a job will turn against the regimes.

The dependency ratio discloses how many people working will have to support the people aged over 65 years. A high dependency ratio indicates that a smaller labour force will have to support a growing number of people who are not taking part in the productive life of the country. More money will be directed to supporting the elderly, crowding out investments in production and research and development. History tells us that no country with a high dependency ratio has been able to maintain high economic growth.

Table 6.2 shows the dependency ratio for China, with the United States and Africa for reference.

China was doing well until the beginning of the twenty-first century, after which the figures gradually turned against the country. Sometime during the 2030s the situation will become worrying, and by 2050 it will be a bomb waiting to go off for the Chinese economy. It will approach a situation not identical to those in Japan and some European countries, but on the same trajectory. The European Union in 2050 will have a dependency ratio of 48 per cent, and the ratio for Japan will be as high as 74 per cent.[6]

India will not feel the burden of the dependency ratio until around 2050, and even then it will be much easier for it to manage than is the case for China. The implication of the dependency ratio is that China

TABLE 6.2
Percentage Share Of Those Aged 65 To Those Aged 15–64

Region/Year	2005	2020	2050
United States	18	24	34
China	11	17	39
India	8	10	21
Africa	6	7	11

needs to invest in order to finance a much larger welfare burden, whilst India can wait with no need to pay much attention to this aspect until 2050. Hence, China's interest in investing in India's transformation, and India's ability to borrow and service the debt in view of a large and rising labour force and low dependency ratio.

Taken together, the size of the labour force and the dependency ratio tells us that China had reaped the demographic dividend until the turn of the century, and will be able to manage until the mid-2030s. Sometime around 2035 the established model will no longer be able to take the country ahead. China must prepare for a shift in the economic paradigm. Searching for alternatives and discussions about which way to go are clearly ongoing. The leadership is probably undecided, and perhaps a little bit in the dark, as there is no tried-and-tested model for it to adopt.

The Japanese experience is not an attractive one for China, if for no other reason than Japan has since 1990 been caught in low growth, which does not seem acceptable for China. Japan has not been able to mobilize its elderly population. The use of robotics has somewhat alleviated the social problem of caring for the elderly, but the main challenge is to reintegrate them into the labour force, and neither Japan nor any other country has found the key to do this. Tepid attempts have been made in Europe to lift the retirement age by a couple of years. This has helped a little, but not much. In China, with the problem of the gigantic scale, the need to square this circle seems unavoidable, for it to find a middle way between retirement and staying part-time, or whatever term can be invented, to remain at the disposal of the labour market.

It is possible that the Chinese look towards India with a certain amount of envy, seeing their large neighbour is going to reap the demographic dividend in the future. But then, China had enjoyed this tailwind from 1979 to the turn of the century, and had used it wisely to propel itself forward.

The United States falls between China and India. Its workforce will increase from 195 million in the year 2000 to 240 million by 2050. Unfortunately, the dependency ratio for the United States will also increase, from 18 per cent to 34 per cent. On both points it is doing better than China, which could weigh against China's efforts to overtake the US economy. It is difficult to see how a country with a negative demographic outlook could gain ground in terms of GDP per capita over another with a more favourable demographic outlook.

For the time being, the Chinese perspective seems to be to wait and test the water while investing in the Belt and Road Initiative, to take part in India's transformation as the most important policy response, and to move into high technology as the main competitive parameter.

Technology

China has ratcheted up its expenditure on research and development, pumping US$519 billion (2019) into it, which is close to the US figure of US$581 billion. China's determination and the size of its commitment is illustrated by the gap between it and Japan at number three, with US$193 billion, followed by Germany with US$112 billion and India with US$94 billion.[7]

Several indicators hint at China's already strong position.

The number of patents may not necessarily reveal the technological strength of a nation-state, but it is nevertheless an indicator of the amount of its research and development. In 2006, Asia accounted for 49.7 per cent of patents filed globally. In 2016, the figure was at 64.6 per cent, with China by far in the lead.[8] For international patent applications filed via the World Intellectual Property Organization (WIPO) (2017), China trailed only the United States. WIPO forecasts however that in less than three years China will be in first place. Huawei and ZTE were the two top corporations filing international patents.[9]

UNWIPO, Cornell University and INSEAD have since 2007 published a Global Innovation Index. In 2007 the United States ranked at the top in this index, and China was number 27, behind India and Malaysia. In 2018 the United States was number 6, while China had moved up to number 17.[10]

The journal *Nature*—the premier international journal of the sciences—compiles an index of scientific papers published in the top eighty-two journals. It concluded that from mid-2017 to mid-2018, China had closed the gap with the United States, accounting for 13,434 of the papers, with the United States standing at 26,623. These figures may underestimate the gap, as almost all the articles classified as Chinese were written by Chinese citizens in China, while a considerable number of articles classified as American were written by foreigners who had emigrated to the United States or who stay there temporarily.[11]

In the last decade of the twentieth century, China ranked sixth on a list of countries conducting joint studies with the United States. In the first decade of the twenty-first century, it ranked number one.[12]

Five main programmes characterize China's efforts to gain the technological edge.

A gigantic plan to boost mass entrepreneurship and innovation has been launched to engineer a structural shift from an industrial economy to a service-based one, underpinned by technology and innovation.[13] It has been alleged that US$320 billion will be used to implement the programme.

"Made in China 2025" is aimed at upgrading China's production from labour-intensive, low-cost manufacturing to products with a higher degree of value added. It also aims to raise the percentage of domestic core materials to 40 per cent in 2020 and to 70 per cent by 2025. The plan was apparently inspired by the German blueprint for Industrie 4.0, and it has led to raised eyebrows in the United States and Germany, who see it as a strategic manoeuvre to overtake them in value-added manufacturing.[14]

Artificial intelligence (AI) is the battering ram in the Chinese arsenal. In 2017 the government defined three targets: keeping pace with AI technologies in 2020, achieving AI breakthroughs by 2025, and being the world leader by 2030. In 2017 China accounted for close to half of global venture capital that went into AI. The country's main advantage is the mass of data it has available, not least of which is that produced from the drive towards a cashless society, which engineers a colossal amount of data.[15]

Biotechnology and genetic engineering are at the forefront, with the government identifying pharma and biotech as the two main pillars of future economic growth. AI and the mass of data can also help to promote this sector. In 2017, US$30 billion was raised by biotech start-ups; for the first half of 2018 the figure was US$32 billion.[16]

Sustainability and the circular economy—primarily aimed at a high degree of recycling of solid waste—is linked to improving the environment and reducing pollution. The thirteenth five-year plan for 2016–20 contains specific proposals that target recycling and the fight against pollution. The background to this was the prognosis that pointed to twenty-five per cent of all global waste coming from Chinese municipalities by 2025.[17] As is the case in the EU, there is an understanding in China that solid waste is a potential source of wealth that, if managed correctly, may be turned into an asset for the economy.

The question is whether the Chinese leadership understands that such a transformation is not only about political will and money but about changing the mindset of people, and even more so about providing a large social and educational infrastructure. The innovations may be forthcoming, but will China have the accompanying services that will allow ideas and innovations to flourish and to transit from the drawing board to actual production, resulting in a large number of major enterprises offering jobs for the population? Will the education sector be able to tap into this process and offer education that will provide the skills that will be in demand? The United States mastered this game because it was a holistic society, where the market mechanism ensured that accompanying services emerged when needed. This is not something that can be done via economic plans. It needs to happen by itself, as entrepreneurs spot the opportunities and the regulatory system helps them to transform ideas into realty.

The human factor and the interaction between people, business and government may be a more decisive factor than the leadership having the right ideas.

Energy[18]

A seminal shift is taking place as the United States moves from being the third-largest importer of fossil fuels in 2013 to becoming a net exporter by 2023, and from 2018 being a net exporter of liquified natural gas.[19]

The future game will mainly be about gas, where the United States is the biggest consumer and will continue to be so leading into 2040. US production, however, will be higher than domestic consumption, forcing it to seek customers abroad. The biggest fossil fuel market for a horizon 2040 projection will be China. India will show the highest growth in demand, but from a much lower starting position.

The supply-demand equation for the coming years predicts a buyer's market, with a large number of countries—the United States among them—either entering the market or hiking production. No one is waiting eagerly to buy US gas. In order to get a reasonable price for its gas, the United States will need to do two things. First it will try to squeeze some of the existing suppliers out, which explains its policy towards Iran and Qatar, as it would be convenient if these two suppliers were not allowed to sell on the market. Secondly, it will try to get into the Chinese market, which is one of the reasons the Trump administration talked about using the trade war as an instrument to get China to buy more gas from the United States.

The major shift connotes that the United States as a net exporter has changed its geopolitical interests, leading it to break up alliances. As a net importer, the United States had shared interests with the other net importers in Europe, Japan and Korea. They were all core countries in the alliance system. The United States was prepared to adopt a foreign and security policy that ensured they could all continue to import fossil fuels, and the only region capable of delivering this supply was the Middle East. It was therefore crucial to maintain peace and stability there; or, rather, to ensure that the United States was the ultimate power broker. The sea lanes across the Indian Ocean, the Strait of Malacca and the South China Sea must remain open to prevent Japan or Korea being cut off from their energy supply. As a net exporter, the United States is asking itself why it should pay for peace in the Middle East to avoid conflicts that would disrupt production and keep sea lanes open. Instead, an alliance with Saudi Arabia might be envisaged. With that country being the biggest supplier of oil and the United States being the biggest supplier of gas, some kind of unholy alliance could make sense for both of them.

China's interests are to ensure it will not be cut off from external energy supplies. This is one of the reasons it is boosting nuclear energy and renewables, as these are under its own control. China has also diversified its energy imports. The top five countries that China buys crude oil from (2018) are Russia, Saudi Arabia, Angola, Iraq, and Oman. The United States is number ten.[20] The top five suppliers of natural gas (2017) are Turkmenistan, Australia, Qatar, Malaysia, and Indonesia. The United States is number nine.[21]

China will certainly not make itself dependent on the United States as a supplier of gas coming from the fracking boom, but the figures indicate there is scope for a hike in the share of imports from the United States, which can be made use of in adroit geopolitical manoeuvres.

While the swing in the US position from net importer to net exporter breaks up alliances and plays an important role in its geopolitical posture, the opposite is the case for China. Its dependence on energy imports lies behind a strong effort to build partnerships.

The government-owned State Grid of China is building a gigantic transmission grid across the country, linking the far west with the coastal cities. It has a capacity of 1.1 million volts. It will enhance energy efficiency and have a positive effect on sustainability, as energy can be transported to where the need is, which solves at least part of the problem connected with the storage of wind power. The ambition, however, does not stop there. State Grid envisage a transmission net, linking adjacent countries to a vast grid that can shuffle energy among countries dependent on production and demand. It can be classified as part of the Belt and Road Initiative. State Grid is investing in Australia, Greece, Italy, the Philippines and Portugal, and is active in Egypt, Ethiopia, Mozambique and Pakistan. It is the largest power distributor in Brazil.[22]

Demographics, Technology and Energy

These three steering factors for the 2035 global outlook all unequivocally augur fundamental change. They all constitute a break with the past.

All three interact with each other. The demographic situation forces China to invest a major stake into technology, provoking a reaction from America. At the same time, China and India will need to cooperate in the relocation of labour intensive, low-cost manufacturing from China to India. The two Asian giants, along with Japan and South Korea, continue to be net importers of fossil fuels, while the United States has switched to being a net exporter and is looking to export gas to them. While these nations welcome buying from the United States, they do not want to depend on it, and this is pushing them into diversifying imports. This has the potential to annoy the United States, and it is setting Russia and the United States up against one other as they look for markets in the energy game.

The power game will be concentrated in Asia, home to the four main importers of fossil fuels. It will take place among the strongest economies, and will see determined efforts to develop advanced technological solutions. These elements entail the risk of triggering a conflict, but it is unlikely to be of military character. The awareness of this risk should hopefully induce the main players to manoeuvre carefully in order to prevent such an outcome.

Key Points

The previous chapter analysing the global financial crisis concluded that the United States no longer possess the strength or willpower to be a global superpower, able to take the lead and act as the guarantor—the underwriter—of the system.

This chapter shows that the three big sinews of global economics and power-related effects favour China, but this situation is not without its caveats. China's demographics will turn against it around about 2035. Technology could possibly become the main competitive parameter, but the way ahead for China will not be without problems or challenges, especially when it comes to competing with the United States for the technological edge. China may do well, and with luck technology will underpin reasonable growth for it. But it is doubtful whether China will be able to build the accompanying services and the supporting environment to be able to propel it to the number one position in terms of global technological power. Energy is a weak point for China, as it will continue to be a net importer on a large scale, forcing it to use energy as an instrument in foreign and security policy. This may help it to shape alliances—as was the case for the United States until it turned the tables and became a net exporter—but it will be a drain on the economy.

This picture casts doubt over the continuity we have seen between 1945 and 2010 of an uncontested superpower capable and willing to project power globally. In the mid-2030s, neither the United States nor China will possess the strength to be a global leader. The responses to the changing situation by the two countries seem to have been different: the United States has moved to break up alliances, whilst China has sought to development new partnerships.

Something else will shape economic globalization and the power game. It looks likely that regionalization will replace globalization.

Notes

1. If not stated otherwise, sources for demographics are publications from the United Nations Population Division.
2. *The Economist*, Economic and Financial Indicators.
3. https://www.investindia.gov.in/team-india-blogs/india-china-investment-corridor-dangal-and-business-goes-hand-hand.
4. Ibid.
5. Betty Hung and Lee Xian, "China I ODI from the Middle Kingdom: What's Next after the Big Turn Around?", BBVA Research, 13 February 2018, https://www.bbvaresearch.com/en/publicaciones/china-odi-from-the-middle-kingdom-whats-next-after-the-big-turnaround/.
6. Commission of the European Communities, *Regions 2020: Demographic Challenges for European Regions* (Brussels: Commission of the European Communities, 2008), p. 3.
7. These figures are not fully compatible with those provided for R&D in chapter 2. https://www.statista.com/statistics/732247/worldwide-research-and-development-gross-expenditure-top-countries/.
8. http://www.wipo.int/edocs/pubdocs/en/wipo_p..ub_941_2017.pdf.
9. Friederich Wu, "Introducing the World's *New* Technology Leader", *International Economy* (Winter 2019): 66.
10. Ibid.
11. Ibid.
12. *Nikkei Asian Review*, 22 May 2014.
13. See, for example, newspaper reports on the programme trying to mobilize China's mass of talent. http://www.chinadaily.com.cn/a/201809/07/WS5b91cc35a31033b4f4654b65.html.
14. For a brief description, see https://en.wikipedia.org/wiki/Made_in_China_2025.
15. https://www.cnbc.com/2018/12/14/china-could-surpass-the-us-in-artificial-intelligence-tech-heres-how.html.
16. https://asia.nikkei.com/Spotlight/Cover-Story/China-s-great-leap-forward-in-biotech.
17. For a brief description, see https://en.wikipedia.org/wiki/China%27s_Circular_Economy.
18. If not stated otherwise, the source for the energy statistics is the *World Energy Outlook* of the International Energy Agency (IEA).
19. US Energy Agency Administration.
20. http://www.worldstopexports.com/top-15-crude-oil-suppliers-to-china/.
21. https://asia.nikkei.com/Business/Markets/Commodities/China-on-pace-to-become-top-natural-gas-importer-in-2018.
22. https://www.technologyreview.com/s/612390/chinas-giant-transmission-grid-could-be-the-key-to-cutting-climate-emissions/.

7

Globalization to Regionalization

Indicators of a New Power Structure

International *trade* used to be global, as the label "the global supply chain" indicates, but it is turning into a regional supply chain. No other place demonstrates this phenomenon as clearly as Asia. Asia's share of intraregional trade was 57.3 per cent in 2016, up from an average of 55.9 per cent between 2010 and 2015.[1] It has been a general pattern, when analysing global trade, that trade among emerging markets and developing economies has been increasing, while that among industrialized countries has been in decline. What may be termed south–south trade had increased from 8 per cent of global trade in 1995 to 20 per cent in 2016. In contrast, north–north trade has fallen from 55 per cent in 1995 to 33 per cent today.[2]

At first glance this may not seem much. But if the trend continues, and all signs indicate that it will, it is going to turn the tables of the global trade structure. It shows that whilst Asia in the past produced for consumption in the United States and Europe, it is now producing for consumption in Asia. From a logistics and transport point of view, the supply chain is becoming more compact, which will have repercussions on international transport, mainly sea transport, and in particular on container lines, which will need to adjust after decades of investment in global transport.

The global value chain is replacing the global supply chain as an indicator of the complexity of global trade. One example is that fifteen thousand components come together to make up a modern car. More than two-thirds of international trade—including the supply of smartphones, cars, TVs and computers—takes place within such global value chains. It allows each country to specialize in a particular role or phase of the chain. China, for example, exports many technological products, but it has in fact moved into the role of an assembler of components from many other countries, including the United States, sitting at the end of many global value chains.[3]

The position of a country—its diversity and competitiveness—can be measured by its integration into the global value chain, which reveals how much of its exports are used by other countries as intermediate goods for their own exports (forward integration) and how much of its imports are used as intermediate goods for its own exports (backward integration). The higher the share of total trade is, the more sophisticated a country's economy is and the more it is integrated in the supply chain, thereby playing the value-added card.

In 2017, the US share of this was 46.5 per cent (13.3 per cent for backward integration and 33.2 per cent for forward integration); for China it was 44.4 per cent (12 per cent for backward integration and 32.4 per cent for forward integration). The interpretation is that China's economy is close to being as sophisticated and linked to the global value chain as that of the United States.

It is worthwhile to dig a little deeper to see which countries the United States and China are most heavily engaged with. They do not interact much with each other. Out of total trade, the share of US value-added trade with China is 3.1 per cent, and China's value-added trade with the United States stands at 2.6 per cent. Both countries are strongly integrated with the European Union—with a share of 16.2 per cent for the United States and 17.1 per cent for China. The intraregional aspect is seen when looking at Mexico and Canada for the United States, which account for 11.6 per cent, and by looking at the rest of Asia for China, which accounts for 12.5 per cent. The difference between the United States and China in their respective integration with adjacent countries (intra-regional) may not be so big, but it is significant in comparison with how little they integrate with each other. Behind these figures is the fact that China exports goods for consumption to the United States and engages in a value chain with the rest of Asia to do so. It buys intermediate goods from the rest of Asia in order to manufacture the final goods for export.[4]

China's role can be illustrated by looking at how large a share of its exports to the United States include Chinese components. Analyses conclude that the value-added content has probably been increasing over time. In 2015 it stood at slightly under 25 per cent. At one point it might have been only 20 per cent. For the Apple iPhone, it is less than 5 per cent. It is quite low, and much lower than US exports of goods to China.[5]

The swing to Asia is similarly visible when looking at *international investment* (incoming investment to a country), or foreign direct investment (FDI), and a country's investment in other countries, or outgoing direct investment (ODI). Intraregional FDI in Asia rose from 48 per cent of the total in 2015 to 55 per cent in 2016. These figures may be volatile, but there is no doubt about the trend, which is moving in the same direction as the case for trade.[6]

Comparing the United States and China as global investors, the following picture emerges. China ranks as the third-largest according to net international investment position (NIIP). Its ODI surpasses its FDI, with US$1.7 trillion (16 per cent of GDP). The United States is the biggest global debtor country.[7]

The total global stock of FDI can be estimated at US$22 trillion. The US share is 25 per cent, with an estimate for China of 5 per cent. The flow of FDI in 2017 can be estimated at US$1.7 trillion, with China accounting for 10 per cent. As the figures show, China is slowly increasing its share of total global FDI. But even with a flow at double this rate, it will take a long time before China reaches the level of the United States.[8]

The two countries are leaders in terms of being recipients of FDI. The US receives 18–19 per cent of the share, whilst China accounts for 10 per cent. The continued attractiveness of the United States is explained by its economy being larger than China's, by its capital market and its technological edge.[9]

They do not invest as much in each other's economies as the media would have us think. In 2017 the stock of US ODI accumulated in China was estimated at US$250 billion, equivalent to 1.2 per cent of total US ODI. The reason for this low amount may be that the United

States only started to invest in China a couple of decades ago, whilst it has been investing in the rest of the world for more than a hundred years. China's stock of ODI going to the United States is complicated to estimate because it depends on how Hong Kong is classified, but a rough calculation gives a figure of 4 per cent of its total ODI.[10]

On 26 June 2015 the *Financial Times* quoted research predicting that China's offshore assets would rise from US$6.4 trillion to nearly US$20 trillion by 2020.[11] Such a rise implies a colossal savings surplus to be invested abroad. China's savings surplus reached 9.9 per cent of GDP in 2007, but it has fallen steadily since.

This and other analyses and forecasts for China's ODI warrant a closer look at *where the ODI is actually going*, with a view to assessing whether China can turn itself into a genuine global investor or whether it will focus on ODI in Asia.

China's ODI in the United States is not, as often described by media reports, concentrated in high-tech sectors. The top five sectors (2017) are real estate, transport, information and communication technology, health, and financials. ODI going to aviation, machinery and electronics are all negligible compared to the top sectors, and less than, for example, entertainment. The top sectors for US ODI going to China are information and communication technology, entertainment, automobiles, food and agriculture, and real estate.[12]

The flows of Chinese global ODI between 2005 and 2017 reveal that, over this twelve-year period, commodities and energy were dominant, accounting for close to 50 per cent of the total. Technology did not represent a steady trend, being almost absent in some years and rarely registering more than 10 to 15 per cent of the total.[13] For 2016–17, Europe was the biggest recipient, with Asia coming second. Countries participating in the Belt and Road Initiative (BRI) saw their share of total ODI increase to 12 per cent. The United States came in as the third-highest recipient. The four main categories to all countries were commodities, energy, transport, and logistics.

Looking at Southeast Asia as an example of Chinese ODI in Asia, an increase is visible. But the traditional investors—Europe, the United States and Japan—are still far ahead. For 2007–16, China was the fourth-largest investor, with 5 per cent of total FDI in the region. Lately, the Chinese share has risen to about 10 cent, but this is still behind Europe at 31 per cent and the United States and Japan both with

11 per cent.[14] Government infrastructure in ASEAN attracts money from Japan and China, but even with the Belt and Road Initiative, China is lagging behind Japan, with ODI of US$255 billion from Japan since the early 2000s compared to US$155 from China.[15]

Combining trade and investment, the conclusion is that the United States is losing its preponderant place in the global supply chain while at the same time it still accounts for the largest stock of ODI; its savings deficit means it will not be able to strengthen its position. American companies can and unquestionably will continue to be among the biggest foreign investors, but the United States as a country is running up debt, making its position perilous.

China is favoured by the strengthening of the intraregional trade and investment that is taking place in Asia, with the Chinese economy as its flywheel. The country's falling savings surplus though sets limits on how much it can invest overseas. Chinese companies (private and state-owned) are competing in the government's drive for large and prestigious projects under the Belt and Road Initiative and the State Grid project. In the future, China will need to be more selective and to set its priorities. Figures indicate it will prioritize regional investments. Indeed, analyses published in 2019 reveal that since the BRI began in 2013, China's outward investments in BRI projects have risen faster than the country's total outward investments.[16] Outside Asia, projects linked to the BRI may be more likely to be given the green light. It is beyond China's reach though to become a large overseas investor in the mould of the British Empire or the United States.

Regionalization

The withdrawal by the United States as the guarantor of the global system means other nation-states can no longer rely on it or on the global system designed to project its power—reflecting American values and norms—to solve their problems. The rules-based system has lost its power because no one is willing or capable of enforcing the rules. Indeed, the one that was supposed to do so, the United States, is the one breaking the rules and making a virtue of it.

The fact of trade and investment becoming more regional implies that nation-states increasingly see their economic interests linked with and dependent on the region rather than the global economy. It does not mean that the global system no longer exists or that the global economy has disappeared, but it does mean that the force behind and the interests in safeguarding it have shifted from the global to the regional level.

The ambitious global trade initiatives are at an impasse. The World Trade Organization has not been able to forge an agreement on the Doha Round, covering twenty trade sectors, which was launched in 2001. In reality, the round died in 2008.

The United States launched and subsequently killed the Trans-Pacific Partnership, which was aimed at defining future rules for trade not only in the goods sector but, more importantly, in the services sector. The key sentence in President Obama's opinion piece in the *Washington Post* of 2 May 2016 stated that the economic and political objective was to "make sure we write the rules of the road for trade in the 21st century".[17] Nothing says more about the shift in US policy vis-à-vis economic globalization than comparing this statement to the decision by President Trump to withdraw from the initiative. Its companion, the Transatlantic Trade and Investment Partnership, never looked likely to get off the ground.

Despite the numerous meetings held by the International Monetary Fund, it has never come close to formulating a genuinely global economic policy that would see the main economies working in tandem and supporting one another. Nor, for that matter, has anything of the like been achieved at the meetings of groupings such as the G7 (Canada, France, Germany, Italy, Japan, the United Kingdom and the United States) or the G20 (a larger and broader economic forum that includes nineteen nation-states and the European Union).

Regional initiatives, on the other hand, have seen a tailwind, particularly in Asia. The Regional Comprehensive and Progressive Agreement is largely a Chinese initiative for an enhanced free trade agreement that includes all the large Asian economies (China, Japan, India, Korea, the ten members of ASEAN, Australia and New Zealand). It has profited from the United States abandoning the TPP. So has the Comprehensive and Progressive Agreement for Trans-Pacific Partnership, with a smaller group of countries replacing the TPP and keeping it alive in the hope that the United States will change its mind and join at a later stage. China has launched the Belt and Road Initiative and the Asian Infrastructure Investment bank. In Central Asia, the Shanghai Cooperation has been established with eight members (China, Russia, India, Pakistan, Kazakhstan, Tajikistan, Kyrgyzstan, and Uzbekistan), plus four observers (among them Iran) and six dialogue partners. On top of this, many Asian nations are busy negotiating free trade agreements. Asia has been the centre for this swing towards regionalism, but a similar movement can be seen in other parts of the world.

Weaving geopolitics, economics, trade and investment into the tapestry, three regions now resolve themselves: North America, probably enlarging to include the Western Hemisphere; East Asia, gradually developing into an Asian regional system; and Europe, plus some adjacent countries and areas. Africa may in due course emerge as a fourth region.

The three regions will each be dominated by one country playing the role of "factory" for the region and as the economic powerhouse. In the Western Hemisphere it will be the United States; in Asia, China; in Europe, Germany. They will each play the role of a hub. It is noteworthy that in Asia this role will unreservedly go to China, without Japan being a challenger. This is because the Chinese economy is much more important for the supply chain and the value chain. It is the biggest buyer and seller of intermediate goods. The supply chain has shifted heavily to "factory Asia" from "factory Europe" and "factory North America".[18]

While globalization entailed a mixture of values, economic interests and military security, all inspired by the United States, regionalization will not reflect common or shared values but will rather focus on pursuing certain interests—economic and military—in a more uncertain environment. Values provide a high degree of certainty about behaviour, whilst the pursuit of interests, particularly when this takes place in an untested environment, may lead nation-states to be unpredictable. There are no established rules, so the participants will need to test one another. The relationships between the strongest power and the smaller nation-states will need to adjust, and they will not be easy to predict.

There are several vital questions.

The first is whether it will be possible to shape a rules-based system. Not exactly like the European Union, but something that links members together in a law-based system, including rules for settling conflicts. There are two crucial items to consider. Will member states be willing to tackle decisions with some kind of qualified majority vote, or will they stick to unanimity? In the case of a need for unanimity, there are limits to how much can be done, as any member state can block further progress. The second item to consider is whether in specific areas a pooling of sovereignty can be introduced? If neither of these steps are taken—and it seems doubtful that they will be—the regionalization will be of an intergovernmental character, preventing integration from jumping from primarily trade and possibly services to other sectors.

There is a certain misunderstanding, both in Europe and other parts of the world, about what the concept of sovereignty and its role in economic integration means. In the old days, with a national economy and the nation-state in the driver's seat, sovereignty served to protect the nation-state against unwelcome influences from the outside. It worked because most economic transactions were national, allowing the nation-state to exercise control. It was a defensive policy. In the era of economic globalization—whether globalization or regionalization—this has changed fundamentally. Now, a large proportion of economic transactions are international, evading national control. The only way to maintain some control is to participate actively in the formulation of international rules-making, to ensure such rules include provisions for a nation-state to pursue national policies. This has been highlighted in the Brexit debate, where the slogan of "taking back control" could not be more wrong, as Britain will now become a follower instead of the rule maker it could have been had it stayed in the EU.

Very often the phrase of giving up sovereignty, of losing sovereignty, or of abandoning sovereignty can be heard. That is not a correct interpretation. The basic idea of sovereignty within globalization is that it is *transferred* in order for it to be exercised in common with adjacent nation-states that are pursuing analogous political goals. It is an offensive strategy employed by nation states when they negotiate to write rules so that everybody becomes a stakeholder and benefits from them. It enhances its room to manoeuvre for a nation-state to exercise control over economic transactions that otherwise would be beyond its control—national legislation does not work in an international world; only international legislation does.

In a situation of regionalization that is not rules based, it is very much up to the strongest nation-state to decide the balance between rules and egoistic behaviour. The weaker and smaller nation-states will be more dependent on the strongest one, not only because its economy is so much bigger but also because the alternative of seeking assistance from powers outside the region does not look good. The strongest powers in the regions will respect one another's spheres of interests, and will be reluctant to interfere for fear their opposite numbers in other regions could do the same towards them. The world will come to see what in the business world is called collusion.

It cannot be taken for granted, but the strongest power should see its interest in sharing economic benefits with its partners in order to make sure that everyone would be better off inside rather than outside. It should avoid dividing the members by offering benefits to some but not to all. With such an approach, a fairly robust system could be built where member states would feel sufficiently secure and comfortable.

The smaller and weaker nation-states should devote their attention to how they can make themselves "indispensable" in the regional system; that is, how they can contribute to the economy in a way that not only benefits themselves but which also leaves other member states better off. A move along these lines—like the transfer of sovereignty—is an offensive policy, taken with a clear perception of the country's role in the region, thereby gaining the respect of the strongest nation-state and the friendships of smaller nation-states. Should it instead try to protect itself, the prospects for beneficial economic developments would not be good, as such a country is too small to be able to act alone and would not be able to find alternatives outside the region.

The situation in Asia differs from that in Europe in at least one fundamental respect. There are four "blocks": China, Japan, India, and Southeast Asia. Many observers fear that China will not be a benevolent leader of regionalization, but will be too assertive and heavy handed, monopolizing the power and the benefits. That development is unlikely. If China did head in that direction it would trigger a reaction from Japan and from India and it could stimulate the members of ASEAN to close ranks. None of this would be in China's interests.

The global power structure will adapt to the situation of there being three (or four) regions. The existing international organizations (the International Monetary Fund, the World Bank and the World Trade Organization) will still be there, but they would serve as forums for interactions among the three regions. There will be no interest in shaping a form of global governance because very few will see any gain in genuine globalization in view of trade and investment being more regional than global. The strongest powers will stay away from interfering in the situation inside other regions, and any attempts on the part of smaller nation-states to rally support from the outside will fail. The new reality of the world will be one divided into spheres of interest.

Spheres of Interest

A sphere of interest is often defined as how much territory (land and sea) beyond its borders that a superpower can control or at least have influence over. This was because acts of aggression took the form of armies or navies approaching a power, which would want a buffer zone around it where it could fight defensive battles, and not on its own territory.

During the industrial age, the concept of the sphere of interest gradually became broader to include matters of economics, trade and investment. A superpower needed an outlet for the production of its goods and services in order to achieve economies of scale and at the same time helping to keep challengers at bay. It would need to acquire resources from abroad—even the United States was not self-sufficient in resources—so as to keep the economy running. The idea the British had in the 1930s of creating a system of imperial preferences is an example of how this looks from the angle of policymakers. Imperial Japan's concept of the Greater East Asia Co-Prosperity Sphere prior to and during World War II is another one.

In the era of globalization and regionalization, territory no longer plays a role. Economics does, but to a much lesser extent than it did previously.

What matters today is the capability to create a zone of countries that adopt the same technical standards, use the same technology, exchanging energy through a grid, and belong to the same zone of currency system. It can be formulated in the way that, with technology as the main driver, a group of countries follows the leading nation-state in an interplay of interdependence and dependence. In a regional world, each region will have one or perhaps a limited number of superpowers. They will compete with one another at the global level. The winner—not being a genuine global superpower but rather the primus inter pares—will be the power with the largest mass connected to its technological development. Mass delivers money. And money will continue to be the key instrument in maintaining the technological edge and, as a result, the opportunity to control the global game.

The strongest power in a region will give the smaller member states an offer they cannot refuse. Connect to me on the crucial technological, economic, energy and conceptual items and your economy will flourish; if not, the door to the international economy will be closed. This sounds harsh, but it is mutually beneficial. Both parties get to benefit from economies of scale, albeit on different levels. The superpower receives money for further technological development. The smaller nation-states get access to the superpower's market without any kind of barriers and they may be able to tap into information and communication networks, energy grids and common currency systems, also without barriers. It is reminiscent of the historical kind of patron-client relationship dating back to the Roman Empire—the patron asks for loyalty from its client states, and it offers protection and benefits as quid pro quo.

The competition among superpowers will take place around the following vectors.

The first and most important vector will be *technology*, as the nation-state or group of nation-states that has the technological edge will be able to set the global agenda. At the core of this is control over information and communication technologies—the ability to communicate without interference from outside, to be able to disturb the communication of other nation-states, and to be able to set guidelines for the control over communication to its own citizens.

The United States can be said to be the established power, using the internet to enhance its global power. It is interested in a global network for the simple reason that it started the internet and is home to the biggest companies with regard to both what is offered on the net and how to transport the data (cables). A break-up of the internet would be an enormous setback for American power and it may count more than the balance in military hardware.

China is spearheading an attack by building its own internet. It is in control of what information originating from outside the country can be seen or used by Chinese citizens and the Chinese business sector. Moreover, Chinese apps are fast gaining a foothold in India, Southeast Asia, the Middle East, South America and Africa. Some observers predict that by 2024 the global use of American apps and Chinese apps could be 50:50. Chinese companies such as Tencent and Alibaba are expanding rapidly abroad and are achieving economies of scale to allow them to expand further. Behind this lies the vast amount of data in China that opens the door for Chinese companies to use this competitive parameter to storm ahead of their US competitors.[19] In 2018, former Google CEO Eric Schmidt predicted a bifurcation into a Chinse-led internet and a non-Chinese internet led by America.[20]

China is not the only country that views the global internet, anchored in US standards, as serving American interests, and it is not the only one that is questioning this situation. A number of other countries have begun to look into building their own version of what is sometimes called "The Great Firewall" of China, making it possible to a degree to prevent outside news from entering the country. The task for China is facilitated by having a limited number of entry and exit points to the global internet, while almost all other countries operate a large number of points. Russia is contemplating various ways of doing what China has done, but with the many entry points it has it is unable to emulate the Chinese model.

Certain countries—such as those in a kind of perpetual conflict, like Israel, Ukraine and South Korea, and others aware of threats to their sovereignty—have seen their adversaries weaponize the internet against them. They cannot afford to ignore the threat of being undermined in this way. The obvious first line of defence is to build their own internet, or at least a substitute or partner to the global internet, which would allow them to switch the global internet off should their security interests dictate the need to. None of these nation-states will enter the big game between China and the United States, but their policies show how attitudes to the internet are changing, from being perceived as a unique blessing to something that can be utilized by their enemies.[21]

The race between China and the United States will be determined by who gets the edge with regard to 5G technology and artificial intelligence (AI). For the time being, the United States may be in the lead with respect to AI, but China is pouring money into R&D, and the situation could change in a short span of time.

The jury is still out with regard to 5G, as it is a not simply technology, but rather a combination of technologies and services. The potential applications are therefore not simply questions of technology and hardware but also of the ability to combine various aspects and discern the appropriate opportunities. It appears that China is gaining ground, with Huawei taking the lead. But the United States is fully aware of this and the tables may yet be turned. A sober evaluation of both 5G and AI is that the United States and China are currently racing neck and neck.[22]

These battles are not being fought solely among nation-states; multinational companies have also begun to spy on one another and to hack the digital systems of their competitors to put them out of business, at least for a while. In 2017 the world's biggest container line, Maersk, suffered a cyberattack that forced it to install 4,000 new servers, 45,000 new PCs and 2,500 new applications.[23] Multinationals can act on their own from a purely cynical business perspective, forcing a competitor out of the market for a while and/or imposing high costs on them by forcing them to install new equipment. Multinationals, however, can also act in collusion with nation-states as a tool in the coming power game.

Standards will play a crucial role as countries joining one of these internets may have to accept its specific standards, making it difficult to plug into the internet offered by a competitor.

As for 5G, the race is on between the United States and China. The United States has chosen mmWave, with China going for sub-6. The difference is that sub-6 offers a better range and greater penetration than mmWave—in short, it is better. The American choice was partly dictated by the military, which controls sub-6 and apparently does not want to share it with others, pushing the country into adopting an inferior standard. mmWave also requires a more elaborate infrastructure, which would provide more jobs but at the cost of efficiency. No other country seems interested in mmWave, preferring its competitor sub-6 being offered by China. If this plays out the way it looks like it will, China will sell its version abroad, reap the economies of scale and feed the revenue into further R&D, whilst the United States will be starved of funds as mmWave will only see domestic use.[24]

The Internet Protocol Version represents a similar case. This controls the capacity of the internet. Currently, Internet Protocol Version 4 (IPv4) is in use, but in 2017 China's 751 million users of the internet had only 338 million addresses, which is far too few for their needs. The new version (IPv6) being rolled out will provide a much higher capacity and more addresses. The initiative comes directly from the CPC Central Committee and State Council, and it is not just about making Chinese netizens happier with their internet browsing. The action plan requires that the country uses the next five to ten years to develop the next generation of online autonomous technology systems and the industrial ecology. It will also, according to Liu Dong, president and CEO of BII Group (天地互连), a technical public service platform for internet infrastructure, build the largest IPv6 business application network in the world. "Currently we are experiencing and promoting a fundamental change from the connection of 'people' to the connection of 'things' and this trend will accelerate the era of the Internet of Things [IoT]", Liu said. "IPv6 will become an important support for the IoT era. The resulting massive amounts of data will become an endless source of business value. AI will also change the existing life and production mode by IoT data mining."[25]

According to Liu, IPv6 is an important starting point for the whole online ecosystem, including big data, IoT, cloud computing and other applications. He added that it will promote industrial upgrading of the internet, not just in China but for the whole world. The plan states that the country will have 200 million IPv6 users by the end of 2018, and the number will exceed 500 million by 2020.[26]

Technical standards can be defined as specifications, in the form of rules or guidelines, for materials, products, processes or services. The three "factories" dominating their regions—China, the United States and Germany—will compete to be the number one in smart manufacturing, which relies on highly integrated value chains. It encompasses elements such as cybersecurity, the collection and use of data, digital trade and artificial intelligence.[27]

Each of the three has chosen a different approach to smart manufacturing, with China going for a managed approach, the United States a market-driven one, and Germany a coordinated policy. A global ranking of these three countries reveals that China is number one in value-added manufacturing, with the United States as number two and Germany number three. For value added in manufacturing per capita, China drops to tenth place, with the United States at number four and Germany number one. For manufacturing R&D spend, China is number one, the United States number two and Germany number four.[28]

The problems that China faces in this regard are a limited market and a dependence on foreign technology. The question is whether China can make the transformation into smart manufacturing without moving further towards a market economy and tapping into global consumer demand. For the United States, the problem is a lack of government guidance or leadership, embodying a risk of losing out to competitors abroad, as seems to have been the case for 5G. For Germany, the challenge is a lack of scale, as it is a smaller economy than either China or the United States. However, mobilising the EU could do the trick for Germany.[29]

Next to come are space programmes and the laying of cables, which call for major investments and potential risks. The regional superpower will enlist other nation-states in these programmes, with the quid pro quo that they will get access to these facilities at a favourable price.

In time, technology and the standards connected to their use will shape an extremely strong link among countries in the region, making it almost impossible to break out. Both the superpower and the smaller member states will be captured so to speak in this game. The up side is that it will be mutually beneficial. The price will be unlimited loyalty to the region.

This bond will be strengthened by *trade* and *investment*. Trade liberalization and the rules for investment among members of the region will not be about tariffs, quotas or such similar instruments used as part of trade policy until a couple of decades ago. It will be about technical standards controlling access to markets. They will include environmental and health standards. And they may, deliberately, be different from the standards applied by other regions, in order to strengthen the region and make it more difficult or expensive for outsiders to enter its market. This is borne out by Brexit, where manufacturers in Britain suddenly became aware that components had crossed the Channel several times before the final product was assembled and then often sold on to markets in other EU member states. After Brexit, these components and the final product will be checked at the border to ensure they do not violate the standards applied by the EU.

It will be up to those member-states inside the region to set the rules, and they will of course do so in a manner to enhance their own competitiveness. The rules will be drafted in accordance with what they are best at and in some cases already doing. Their task of adjusting to new standards will be easy. They will also have a time advantage, knowing how the coming standards will look, whilst enterprises outside the region will be part of the process. This is the lesson learned by the Swedish car maker Volvo in the 1980s in competing with car producers inside the EU. It led to a strong drive for Sweden to join the EU, turning Volvo from being a follower of rules to being among the rule makers.

As far as investments are concerned, the trade war between the United States and China shows how rules for foreign investments can be used. China did for many years ask foreign investors to transfer technology, and if they did not acquiesce their investment would be blocked. It proved to be an effective instrument in helping China to close the gap in technology vis-à-vis the United States, being faster and less expensive than to buy the technology or develop it itself.

In today's world, matters of copyright and intellectual property rights have become more and more decisive in the competitive game, and the rules in these areas will form part of a region's panoply of trade and investment instruments.

Energy is fast becoming a policy instrument that is forming alliances and breaking alliances. The United States is breaking up alliances in the slipstream of its transformation from net importer to net exporter. Equally fast, China has been building alliances as the major importer of fossil fuels. India is moving into becoming a large net importer, albeit not of the size of China. Between 2016 and 2040, India's primary energy demand will increase at a rate 25 per cent higher than for China, but this will still leave its total energy consumption at around 40 per cent of the Chinese level.[30] Strategically, this means the two powers will have a common interest in securing imports of fossil fuels, of which they do not have much themselves. This could lead to competition, but it is far more likely they will see interest in cooperating, as competition will drive up prices and hand market control to their suppliers. China's efforts to build a large grid inside and outside China points in that direction.

It is likely that a common energy policy will tackle the question of sustainability and renewable energy, as economic growth not only tends to increase energy demands but also the risk of pollution. The two

Asian juggernauts—China and India; China more so than India—face environmental problems of a size never seen before, and even if they implement policies to reduce pollution, it will take a long time to roll them out and they will cost a lot of money. Building a grid to store energy and to channel it to where peak demand is entails enormous savings and reductions in pollution.

Not far off there will be a shift in the outlook on energy policy, moving it from simply being a tool to keep the economy and indeed society going to integrating it into society and linking it to what is regarded as responsible behaviour with respect to climate change, sustainability and renewable energy. Technology, the Internet of Everything and artificial intelligence may help to mobilize each citizen and every family. The implication is that cooperating about energy will push countries in the region towards a common stance about these issues, further solidifying the links keeping the region together.

Currencies will also be included in this game. As of now the US dollar reigns supreme and it will continue to do so for some time. However, the build-up of regional structures will eventually include some kind of currency cooperation inside the region.

The Europeans discovered that in the long run a single market cannot perform without strong currency cooperation—and that there are no disadvantages to going all the way and creating a single currency. Their experience demonstrated however that the process is more difficult than they had first envisaged. It requires common policies (banking union and fiscal union) and for economic policies to converge, all of which the Europeans balked at in the initial stage, and in the aftermath of the global financial crisis there was further denial.

Currency cooperation inside regions may become some kind of a half-way house, with mutual credit and fixed but adjustable currency rates meaning that member countries will consult with each other before one of them changes its currency rate. There may also be steps towards using other currencies or a basket of their own currencies as a unit of account. In view of the technical difficulties and political obstacles, currency cooperation will probably be the last item on the list linking members of a region together.

The Transition Will Be Dangerous

The global power structure is vulnerable to change. As long as established powers reign, stability is the order of the day. Everybody knows where they stand with one another. Instability takes over when empires break down, as was the case with the Roman Empire, the British Empire and the Chinese dynasties. New powers are eager to test the limits of how far they can go. The previous superpower is no longer there to draw the lines and to step in should they go too far.

This is what will happen when digitalization, demography, technology and energy begin to define a new power structure. Medium-sized powers formerly held back in their ambitions by the United States will now be free to pursue goals that had been out of their reach, and they will encounter other medium-sized powers with similar ideas. The political manoeuvring of Russia, Turkey and Iran demonstrate this. In fact, what has been happening in the Middle East following the Iraq War (2003) is a consequence of a more unpredictable US policy, which has its roots in the decline of US power. The instability in South Asia, although not new, is another example.

The risks of limited wars or military conflicts has risen substantially. This is not necessarily because these powers want war, but rather that they are looking to increase their influence in the region and to possibly extend their sphere of interest without going to war. The crux is that nation-states involved in this new game do not have well-known rules that will allow them to interpret the actions of their neighbours. They may consequently misjudge the steps taken by other countries. The inability to read, convey or understand the signals given may lead to conflicts.

Key Points

The trend in trade and investment favours regionalization. Nation-states will react by gradually giving more emphasis to regional frameworks instead of global rules, although globalization will continue to be important.

Various attempts to form regional frameworks have been seen. Some of them are strong, such as the European Union, which goes beyond simple economics to include political goals and which embodies a transfer of sovereignty to be exercised in common by member states. Others are looser and maintain the intergovernmental structure.

Regions will see spheres of interest dominated by the strongest nation-state or states building a network around technology, trade and investment, energy and currency to create a mutually beneficial system that connects member states to one another, and which will in reality make it impossible for them break out of the region.

An analysis of the future power game between the United States and China illustrates how the lack of power to operate globally has pushed both these nation-states into a regional role.

Notes

1. ADB, *Asian Economic Integration Report 2017*.
2. Jonathan Woetzel, "From Third World to First Class", *Milken Institute Review* (2Q 2019): 22–34.
3. David Dollar, "Invisible Links", *Finance & Development* (June 2019): 50, 53.
4. Unicredit, *Economic Thinking*, no. 76, 7 September 2018; Richard Baldwin and Javier Lopez-Gonzalez, "Supply-Chain Trade: A Portrait of Global Patterns and Several Testable Hypotheses", NBER working paper 18957, April 2013, https://www.nber.org/papers/w18957.
5. Relayed to the author by Professor Lawrence J. Lau of Stanford, who recently published *The China-US Trade War and Future Economic Relations* (Chinese University Press, 2018). See also chapter four, "The Estimation of Domestic Value-added and Employment Induced by Exports: An Application to Chinese Exports to the United States" in *China and Asia: Economic and Financial Interactions*, edited by Yin-Wong Cheung and Kar-Yiu Wong (Routledge, 2009); and "Domestic Value Added and Employment Generated by Chinese Exports: A Quantitative Estimation", *China Economic Review*, 12 April 2012.
6. https://www.adb.org/news/strong-asian-intraregional-trade-and-investment-improve-economic-resilience.
7. https://www.omfif.org/analysis/commentary/2018/july/tale-of-two-creditors/.
8. https://www.brookings.edu/research/united-states-china-two-way-direct-investment-opportunities-and-challenges/; https://rhg.com/research/two-way-street-2018-update-us-china-direct-investment-trends/.
9. Ibid.
10. Ibid.

11. https://www.ft.com/content/5136953a-1b3d-11e5-8201-cbdb03d71480#axzz3e82Rv8Tr.
12. https://rhg.com/research/two-way-street-2018-update-us-china-direct-investment-trends/.
13. https://www.bbvaresearch.com/wp-content/uploads/2018/02/201802_ChinaWatch_China-Outward-Investment_EDI.pdf.
14. *ASEAN Statistical Yearbook 2006–2017.*
15. https://www.bloomberg.com/news/articles/2018-02-08/japan-still-beating-china-in-southeast-asia-infrastructure-race.
16. https://www.straitstimes.com/business/economy/jump-in-chinese-belt-and-road-investment-in-s-e-asia-report.
17. https://www.washingtonpost.com/opinions/president-obama-the-tpp-would-let-america-not-china-lead-the-way-on-global-trade/2016/05/02/680540e4-0fd0-11e6-93ae-50921721165d_story.html?noredirect=on&utm_term=.5964b49f63db.
18. Baldwin and \Lopez-Gonzalez, "Supply-Chain Trade".
19. https://www.cnbc.com/2019/02/04/the-splinternet-an-internet-half-owned-by-china-and-the-us.html.
20. https://www.cnbc.com/2018/09/20/eric-schmidt-ex-google-ceo-predicts-internet-split-china.html.
21. https://www.newamerica.org/cybersecurity-initiative/reports/digital-deciders/ and a good summary http://www.bbc.com/future/story/20190514-the-global-internet-is-disintegrating-what-comes-next.
22. https://www.npr.org/2019/03/11/702355542/the-race-is-on-for-control-of-5g-wireless-communications-and-china-is-in-the-lea.
23. https://www.bleepingcomputer.com/news/security/maersk-reinstalled-45-000-pcs-and-4-000-servers-to-recover-from-notpetya-attack/.
24. https://www.washingtonpost.com/opinions/global-opinions/on-5g-the-united-states-is-building-betamax-while-china-builds-vhs/2019/04/18/1b9cd096-620c-11e9-bfad-36a7eb36cb60_story.html?noredirect=on&utm_term=.998bfe820acd.
25. Masha Borak, "China's Big IPv6 Is Not Just About Faster Internet, It Is About Mass Industrial and IoT Upgrade, *Technode*, 11 December 2017, https://technode.com/2017/12/11/chinas-big-ipv6-push-is-not-just-about-faster-internet-its-about-mass-industrial-and-iot-upgrade/.
26. Ibid.
27. Keith B. Belton, David B. Audretsch, John D. Graham, and John A. Rupp, "Who Will Set the Rules for Smart Factories", *Issues in Science and Technology* (Spring 2019): 70–76.
28. Ibid.
29. Ibid.
30. International Energy Agency (IEA), *World Energy Outlook*.

8

The Power Game in Asia

China Versus the US Regional Powers[1]

An objective of superpower grand strategy is to be seen as strong enough to win a major war, thus precluding the need to actually fight. To make such a policy credible in the eyes of rivals and challengers, the financial strength of the power needs to be solid enough to sustain a protracted war. This includes keeping trade routes open, as a superpower cannot rely over the long term on its domestic resources and production capacity alone. China and the United States have pursued grand strategies that are similar in purpose, but the economic structures, geography and financial constraints limit the global ambitions for each.

Economically, China is much more dependent on access to the global economy than the United States is. China cannot feed itself—the United States is a net exporter of food. China is the largest net importer of fossil fuel—in a couple of years the United States will be a net exporter. China's share of exports/imports to GDP is around 18 per cent—for the United States the figure is around 12–14 per cent (on account of the deficit in the balance of payments, the figure is higher for imports than for exports). According to the OECD, China's outward FDI stands at 14 per cent of GDP and its inward FDI at 21 per cent—the corresponding figures for the United States are 32 per cent and 36 per cent.[2] The United States has been a global investor (outward and inward) for more than a hundred years—China has only participated in this for a couple of decades, which illustrates how quickly China has been building an international investment position.

Geography requires that continental and maritime superpowers react differently to this quandary. A continental superpower, like the former Soviet Union, relies on its neighbours for overland transport links—railways or trucks. A maritime superpower may operate independently of adjacent countries, but it must keep sea lanes open, doing so by naval power.

History does not have any examples of a successful continental superpower operating on a global scale. The closest would be the Roman Empire, extending from present-day Iraq to Portugal and North Africa to the lower Rhine in AD 117. The Spanish, British and American empires were predominantly or exclusively maritime. Challengers like the Soviet Union, Imperial and Nazi Germany, or France under Louis XVI and Napoleon were continental empires that failed in their ambitions of conquest for lack of support from adjacent nations.

China is predominantly a continental power, and it has been so throughout its history, despite a coast that stretches for more than fourteen thousand kilometres. The few examples of Chinese maritime expansion, in particular under Admiral Cheng Ho during the fifteenth century, were brief and took place a long time ago. But despite being a new sea power, China has emerged as a rising superpower that could challenge the United States by land or by sea. Until the Trump presidency, China's leadership may have classified the United States as a reliable partner in the global economy. The recent abrupt shifts in US policies have signalled potential limitations for Chinese exports and investments abroad. Examples include the threat of trade war and the steps taken by several countries to block contracts with Huawei Technologies for 5G networks. China, far from being an autarky, depends on the outside world to support its economy, and it must keep trade routes open irrespective of US policies.

The geography of the situation also highlights the unpleasant fact that the response has been to build an extensive network across the territories controlled by its neighbours, few of which are large trading partners. China shares land borders with fourteen other nations—the longest with Mongolia, Russia, India, Kazakhstan, North Korea, Nepal and Vietnam. This explains the Belt and Road Initiative, an investment programme potentially running close to US$10 trillion. One objective is to secure imports into China of resources, including oil, by building harbours in several neighbouring countries bordering the Indian Ocean or the Bay of Bengal. Another objective is to secure transport corridors for Chinese exports to Asian, European and eventually African nations.

China, fearing a naval blockade in a crisis, plans for transport corridors that will be out of reach of an unpredictable United States. This comes at the price of higher dependence on its neighbours—including Pakistan, Bangladesh, Malaysia and Myanmar. This is a double-edged sword as there is no guarantee that these countries will continue to host the Chinese corridors. Political systems may look stable now, but they cannot be taken for granted. With the global trends of populism and nationalism, regime changes can take place and rulers less likely to be governed by logic and rationality can emerge.

China is fast building a powerful navy, but more than ships will be required in a naval war, especially if the opponent is the United States, which has a long history of sea power and plenty of hard-won experience. For the near future, China will not be able to prevent a US naval blockade. Added to this challenge are the fact of a strong Japanese navy, which is not expected to side with China, and China's dependence on its land-border neighbours. For the time being, this has pushed China towards being more a regional than a global power. China's neighbours may play this game if there are gains to be had from doing so, which will mean that some of the fruits of China's economic growth will fall into their baskets. With the Belt and Road Initiative, China has launched a complicated scheme aiming to shape Asia's future over the coming century. Its success will depend on Asian economic integration producing win-win results for all the countries involved.

The United States may be a continental and maritime superpower, but the balance tilts towards the maritime vector, as Canada and Mexico do not weigh as heavily in the US equation regarding relations with Asia and Europe.

The United States enjoys the luxury of controlling its own destiny with a navy that is sufficiently strong to be able to keep sea lanes open worldwide. When the Japanese naval power began to question US control over the Pacific prior to World War II, the odds for a military conflict rose. The similarity between the British and American empires is striking. In both cases the strategic outlook was to win a naval war against a challenger without losing its role as the dominant global naval power. A predicament emerged for the British at the beginning of World War II when the Royal Navy was still powerful but not powerful enough to take on Germany and Italy whilst at the same time deterring Japan.

Until recently, US dependence reached beyond Asia and Europe because of its net imports of oil, much of it coming from the Arab world. Its Asian allies—Japan and South Korea—also depended to an extent on oil from the Middle East. This explains the US strategic interest in keeping sea lanes open across the Indian Ocean and the South China Sea, instead of confining its strategy to the Pacific. There was a congruity of interests. This dependence on the part of the United States has now fallen to about 20 per cent of its oil needs, whilst the much higher dependencies for Japan and South Korea have not noticeably changed.

Seen from the US-first perspective of the Trump administration, the United States is now less willing to support alliance partners and to secure sea routes for their oil imports. That places a question mark over the value of the Indian Ocean for the United States. Relations with Israel, Arab countries and the base in Qatar may prohibit a strategic downgrading of the Indian Ocean for now, but that may not last for long. The combination of reduced dependence on fossil fuels from the Arab World, the Trump administration's insistence that allies pay for their own defence, and growing debt have cast doubt over whether the United States will maintain its defence spending. The conclusion might well be that trade across the Atlantic and Pacific oceans, but not necessarily the Indian Ocean, will be decisive for the US economy. There may be political reasons for an Indo-Pacific structure, but the economics do not support such a concept.

The America-first point of view of the Trump era may make sense—as elaborate spin that accounts for an inability to continue with US defence expenditures that amount to more than the total combined expenditures of the next seven nations. The US withdrawal from Syria and its reduced military presence in Afghanistan, not to mention talk of the United States leaving NATO, are omens of what is in store. The global superpower is in the process of realigning its commitments to its allies across the globe, bringing them to align with how the US can benefit from the alliance system.

The United States and China are pursuing analogous goals, one of which is to secure trade links. But, because of their distinct geography, they have opted for different strategies, which paradoxically classify both of them as primarily regional rather than global powers.

Asia in the Era of Regionalization

The conceptual framework is that great powers will act in one of three different ways: (1) stabilizing/consolidating, (2) destabilizing/rise/decline, or (3) disruptive. This will depend on where they find themselves in the cycle of great power status. Disruptive or destabilizing influences can be of a domestic origin, they can come from the outside world, or they could come from nature.

Domestic forces such as social instability or an unwillingness on the part of the people to shoulder the burdens and hardships of running an empire may be part of the explanation for the collapse of the Roman Empire. When Britain's manufacturing power waned, it lost a near monopoly of economic power. Other countries (the United States and Germany) took a larger share of global manufacturing, eroding Britain's prerogative.

Many empires succumbed because the elite gradually moved closer to the power centre (king or emperor), leaving the periphery without any links to the centre, and subsequently forgotten and neglected. This played a role in the fall of several Chinese dynasties and of the Spanish Empire. In contrast, the British elite took an active role in building the empire, which is one of the reasons it lasted as long as it did. It is interesting that a large number of the best British generals of World War II began their careers in India, which was the case for Sir Winston Churchill, who arrived in India in 1896 as a lieutenant in the 4th Hussars.

Environmental change may explain the rise and fall of the Mongol Empire, which is often attributed to Genghis Khan but was more likely a result of the climate that made the grasslands of the Mongol steppes green and verdant, fuelling the horses that were the backbone of the empire's military.[3] Climate change also played a role in the decline of the Roman Empire, as the tribes east of its border were forced to move westwards into the empire, which lacked the strength to repel them.

The Angkor-Khmer civilization, which lasted for more than six hundred years, was dependent on water management. It is presumed to have been destroyed by changes in the monsoons.

Political/military/economic changes from beyond the borders of a nation-state can come in the form of other nation-states using new technological advances, such as sea power opening the door for Britain, or the situation at the present of the United States and China vying for the technological edge. Sometimes it could be a combination of two or three factors.

Confrontations can take place when a great power is in decline, trying to defend its established status but without sufficient means to do so. Alternatively, a conflict could arise when a rising power craves recognition but is not acknowledged by the older power. As neither the established power nor the rising one can be certain of their ability to prevail in a conflict, a bluffing game begins, and it can sometimes go wrong. The examples of Britain (and France) vis-à-vis Imperial Germany prior to 1914 and Nazi Germany prior to 1939 illustrate that both sides operated with little knowledge of the opponent's thinking, and what they thought they knew did not fit the reality. (It is often overlooked that in both cases it was Britain that declared war on Germany—not the other way around—and in neither case did Germany expect such a step).

For a declining power, it takes time for a reduced military capability (projection of power) to trickle through. A country's own policymakers and its opponents (potential challengers) tend to act in accordance with power parameters that are out of date—a case of driving using the rear-view mirror. An example of this is Britain in the Far East prior to the Japanese invasion of Malaya, with British policymakers believing the empire had the strength to defend Australia, New Zealand and the colonies. The strategy chosen, however—to only send a naval force to Singapore in case of the threat of war—reflected the reality that the British Empire did not have the money, the manpower or the resources.

Declining powers are aware of the risks of losing their status. Rising powers may in the initial stage be more willing to take risks, as they would have less to lose. In later stages of the power cycle, they will tend to become more risk averse, as they now have more to lose and know how difficult it was to achieve their position. Napoleon took enormous risks in his early days as First Consul and Emperor of

France, only later to be more cautious. As his power grew, he sought to join the European establishment by wedding Princess Marie-Louise of the Habsburg Empire. Hitler likewise took enormous risks in the 1930s. The cases of both Napoleon and Hitler illustrate that a rising power with an unorthodox leadership that adopts different political and military tactics can outmanoeuvre the established powers. But by the same token the results can be short-lived because the established powers learn from and in some cases adopt the same military tactics.

The Soviet Union acted cautiously between 1945 and 1991 because its leadership knew how much it had cost to reach the position it had.

If the stablished power attempts to block or stifle a rising power (by sanctions or trade wars), the new power may resort to conflict, as the alternative would be to back down, which may not be palatable to it. Japan choose to go to war in 1941 when confronted by an oil embargo.

The more confident a power is in its own rights and in the means it has at its disposal, the more predictable its policy steps will be. The United States acted with confidence during most of the Cold War (Berlin Crisis, Cuban Missile Crisis). And the opposite situation was the case for the Soviet Union.

Analysing China, Japan and India under this prism, in addition to Russia and the United States, offers the following observations.

China is a mixture of a destabilizing/rising power and a stabilizing/consolidating power and is acting cautiously to enhance its power and extend its strategic outreach in East Asia. Its tactics are being taken step by step—taking care not to take too long a step or to go for "a bridge too far". it is clearly acting to assert its role, but it is not risking any conflict to do so.

Japan is a stabilizing power with a much lower profile. It does not wish to change the status quo, and it would not know what to do should any other power in Northeast Asia choose to do so.

India is slowly entering the phase of a slightly destabilizing/rising power, but it does not have any confidence in its own capability to assert influence beyond South Asia, so lacking this it is still a stabilizing power.

Russia is a power in Asia, but it is not an Asian power, and it is only a weak power. It can be classified as a disruptive power; able in some cases to block other powers from setting the scene, but not itself able to shape events.

The United States used to be a stabilizing/consolidating power, but it is gradually changing into a disruptive power, not knowing how to maintain its role in Asia or to define what that role should be, thereby sowing uncertainty/unpredictability among its allies and its opponents.

The three great Asian powers—China, Japan and India—will face a *Sino-centric power structure in Asia*. The question is, how will China, as the strongest power, along with Japan and India, who are also big powers but not as big or strong as China, cope with such a situation.

All three countries see themselves as immune from attack from either of the other two. This is largely on account of history and a lack of interest in pursuing such a course, but geography may also be an important factor. The Sea of Japan serves as a barrier between China and Japan, as does the Himalayas between China and India. Japan and India share the feeling that China is a nuisance, an irritant and an assertive power, but not a threat. Only one matter is of such vital interest that it could lead to war, and that is water. If China begins to divert water from the Tibetan Plateau to flow to China instead of India, it would be a question of survival for India to respond. It is very unlikely that China would take such a step, knowing what the reaction from India would be.

A US-led *alliance against China*, encompassing democracies in Asia and Oceania, with India, Japan and Australia usually on the list, is an idea that is often mentioned. These four countries, however, do not have an analogous strategic outlook, apart from a certain sceptical attitude vis-à-vis China, which would not be enough to form an alliance that obviously would have consequences for their relationship with China. The United States would see the other three as pawns in its game vis-à-vis China, and what would India, Japan or Australia gain by that? Particularly in view of the US "withdrawals" from alliances and commitments that have turned it into an unpredictable, almost a destabilizing, power. Trump's policies vis-à-vis Iran and North Korea have come at a price—credibility has been lost!

The pivot or rebalancing to Asia undertaken by the Obama administration was broadly speaking welcomed by most Asian nations, who saw the US presence since the end of World War II as having had a benign impact. The United States had contributed to peace and stability, and almost every Asian nation during the Obama administration would have preferred that the United States continued to stay for a good period to come. But the erratic foreign policy of the Trump administration has left it uncertain as to whether it will. For most Asian nation-states, the policy objective has been to maintain good relations with both the United States and China, and to not be pushed into choosing one over the other. This poses limits for US policy in Asia. A US confrontation or trade war with China is not what Asia wants. The wish is for a good US-China relationship accompanied by US presence in Asia, acting as a counterweight to the rising Chinese influence. This would contribute to a stable power balance in the region, allowing shifts to take place but only gradually and over time, allowing time for the Asia nation-states to adjust.

There is a fundamental difference in strategic outlooks between the United States on the one hand and its allies (Japan and Korea) and potential new allies (such as India) on the other. The United States is not geographically situated in Asia, and is a long way from China. It has the option of withdrawing from a potential conflict without any other loss than prestige and global influence. China may be seen as problem number one—a challenger to America as a global superpower—but it is not vital to US survival. The Asian nations are necessarily in Asia, and in many cases they are neighbours to China. They cannot withdraw. They need to craft a policy that ensures their survival, however strong China may turn out to be.

This difference in outlook can be demonstrated by looking at the foreign policies of Japan and India

Japan's main strategic challenges are matters of military/security via stability on the Korean Peninsula. The dilemma is that a belligerent North Korea poses a risk, but it also serves to maintain the American military presence (including their nuclear weapons) in North East Asia, giving credence to the Treaty on Mutual Cooperation and Security between the United States and Japan. Any fundamental change in the established picture will force Japan into rethinking its basic strategy for its security.

Japan's foreign policy has since 1945 been reactive and extremely cautious. Japan will be immensely reluctant to rely on an American alliance against China (the defence agreement to defend Japan is welcome, but it is not seen as an instrument to contain China). Japan knows China. It may not like what it sees, but that will not lead it into entering an alliance against China. The future relationship between the two will be predictable as long as China is a stabilizing power. For Japan to integrate into a Sino-centric world may not be as difficult as it looks at first glance. China and Japan may vie for influence on the Korean peninsula, but both want a stable situation, and neither of them can get the upper hand—the Koreans will see to that. Economically, China needs Japan as a supplier in its moves into advanced technology, opening the window for Japan to exercise some leverage over Chinese economic and trade policies. It will never be an equitable partnership, but it may be less one-sided than the US-Japan relationship. The Japanese corporations will know that it is in their interest to live in a Sino-centric world, which, in view of economic growth in other areas of the world, offers the only prospect for profitability.

India's main military/security strategic challenge is to be the dominant power in South Asia and to prevent competing powers (primarily China) from gaining too strong a foothold through its bases in the Indian Ocean. India is not strong enough to control the Indian Ocean, but it might be strong enough to prevent its strategic competitors from threatening it from the sea, allowing it some strategic leverage. Many countries use the Indian Ocean for transit, which prevents India from moving into a controlling role, as those wanting it to be open would react. Even if the changing picture for oil and gas from the Middle East has reduced its interests in the Indian Ocean, the United States still has a strong role and bases there (Camp Justice on Diego Barcia), and is not disposed to allow another power to gain naval superiority.

India has a long tradition of non-alignment, and it has deliberately diversified when buying weapons from abroad. It has close links to Russia. In 2018, despite US attempts to thwart the deal, India bought an S-400 missile system from Russia for US$5 billion. India is the largest buyer of weaponry globally, with Russia accounting for 62 per cent of its supplies, followed by the United States at 15 per cent, and Israel at 11 per cent.[4] It has also bought weapons from Sweden, and in 2015 it decided to buy thirty-six Rafale fighter jets from France.

Contrary to the US sanctions on Iran, India has continued to import oil from it as its second-biggest buyer (China is number one). To engage in an alliance with the United States, which is on the opposite side of the globe and which has an agenda that is out of synch with Indian policies, would seem not to be on the table. While China has a global and indeed a regional strategy communicated through various initiatives, India has not. A clash about who is shaping Asia's future would be unlikely in the foreseeable future. The psychological barrier for deepening relations with China may, however, be higher than for Japan. China is essential for India for it to be able to develop into a manufacturing nation. The success of India in this regard is definitely in China's interest, but it is not imperative. The wild card for India is the matter of economic and trade links with the Arab World, Africa (East Africa) and Iran. These links are substantial, but they are unlikely to offer a platform for a transition into manufacturing, which is what India is looking for. The political problem is that some segments of India's political and business world may see it as a genuine alternative.

In terms of foreign policy, Japan and India may both look on China with apprehension. But the main difference in outlook that will have inevitable repercussions on policy is that historically Japan has experience of conflicts with China, whilst India has not.

Economics also separates them in both outlook and policies. The first point to note is the problem of demographics. Japan has to manage a demographic meltdown. By the year 2050, 42.4 per cent of the Japanese population will be over sixty years of age. This is the highest figure worldwide.[5] India will be reaping the demographic dividend until around 2050. India's domestic problem is the need to industrialize in order to provide jobs. The countryside is becoming restless on account of economic pressure. A total of 830 million people (69 per cent of the population) live in the countryside. In 2014, Prime Minister Modi promised to double farm income. He repeated the pledge during the 2019 election, with 2022 set as the target date, but it does not look feasible, which is sowing discontent among a huge mass of the people.

This will almost inevitably colour not only economic policy but also the strategic outlook. There is actually not much congruity to support trade. India and Japan each rank around fifteenth place on the list of each other's trading partners. As for foreign direct investment, while Japan may see it as attractive to invest in India to make good use of cheap labour and to sell to the Indian market, many investors have discovered that it is easier said than done. Partly on account of its status as what has been described as a semi-federal nation, the Indian economy looks larger than it actually is, as each state pursues its own goals and interests. The two can and will certainly continue to build a good relationship, but a kind of alliance that would mainly be directed against China does not seem to be in the offing.

Much will, however, depend on Chinese policy, and in particular how it negotiates the Regional Comprehensive and Progressive Agreement and how it manages the Belt and Road Initiative. If other Asian countries get the impression—rightly or wrongly—that China sees these initiatives as instruments for accruing benefits for itself and as a vehicle to achieve a dominant position in Asia, the prospects for a benign Sino-centric Asia will not be good. If, on the other hand, China realizes and manages to convince its neighbours that its policies are for the mutual benefit of an Asian kind of integration, it may well emerge, securing peace and stability. It will call for a good deal of statecraft, the ability to read the mindsets of other nation-states and to understand their interests.

Relations with the member nations of ASEAN in Southeast Asia can serve as a weathervane. For China, it might be tempting for it to play a divide-and-rule game, trying to split the ASEAN members and deal individually with each of them. There have been signs of such an approach over the last decade. It will, however, be a short-sighted gain, as other ASEAN members may be wary of China's intentions. India and Japan see this as a heavy-handed approach that demonstrates an attempt to play nations against each other. ASEAN can play a role in shaping Asia's future by sticking together and negotiating from a common position, with the chance to emerge as a partner on almost an equal footing with China, India and Japan.

China, Japan and India: Mutual Opportunities and Needs

All three of these nations will be confronting significant economic problems between now and 2035–40, which may call for major policy decisions or even a change in the economic model. They will need each other in order to get through this phase without economic suffering. None of them can rely on the United States.

China needs Japan as a source of high-tech products for the transformation of China into high-tech manufacturing. It needs India for labour-intensive, low-cost manufacturing, with China retaining some control over this through investments.

Japan needs China as a market for its investment goods. India is also expected to be a good market, although not as important as China.

India needs help from China for it to transform into a manufacturing country; it needs China's experience and its assistance in training and in developing the country's infrastructure. Further down the road it will also serve as a market. And Japan will be an investor.

Reason, logic and mutual interests point to Japan and India entering into a Sino-centric world in Asia, provided that China plays its hand wisely and abstains from steamrolling or heavy-handed behaviour, and is willing to share the benefits. Japan and India are too big to accept China as an uncontested leader, but they are not strong enough to craft alternative strategies that could be attractive to other Asian countries.

What may help this to proceed is that Asia is not confronted with foreign or security problems that pitch large countries against one another. Nor do any of the countries of Asia possess the strength to play a genuine global role. It looks like a situation of primus inter pares.

A fairly loose cooperative framework (such as RCEP) will provide sufficient cooperation in economics and trade for at least a while. With a bit of luck, all the partners may see it as a win-win situation, without calling for sacrifices or being restrained by obligations to pursue domestic policies.

A degree of psychological and political resistance will be there that could rock the boat, but presuming that "nations do not have permanent partners; they have permanent interests", such feelings should not overrule Japan and India from joining a Sino-centric world.

On balance, Japan and India may pay a higher price than China should relations sour. It would lead to the following:

- Japan retreating into a self-defined shell. Probably being more nationalistic. Looking at alternative partners in the big league, it is difficult to see who could fit that bill and offer Japan comparable benefits.
- India slowing down entry into economic globalization, and probably questioning economic reforms and the policy to turn itself into a manufacturing nation. There are alternative partners: the Arab World, Africa, and perhaps Russia, but none of these can offer what India's Asian neighbours can. Furthermore, Asian integration would not seem to stand in the way of deepening economic and trade links with countries outside Asia. Because of

its GDP per capita, the situation of its trade and investment, and (not least) its geography and history, India is more unpredictable than either China or Japan. But it would be a decade or perhaps more before India would be able, should it so choose, to put a spanner in the works.
- China trying to live with lower economic growth and a slower transition to advanced technology. The risk is that without a partnership with Japan and India, economic growth may slow down sufficiently to exacerbate social problems

Key Points

Many analyses about Asia's future have focussed almost exclusively on China, taking it for granted that it will be by far the strongest power. A closer look reveals that China needs other Asian nations as much as they need China.

A four-block constellation—China, India, Japan and Southeast Asia—may be wishful thinking, but the facts reveal that mapping out a course benefitting all of them within a frame of Asian integration is preferable to not doing so.

China will be the strongest nation-state (a Sino-centric Asia), and the other Asian nation-states will need to find a way to live with that. China also needs to decide how it will play its cards.

The reason that this scenario is more likely than not is that basically all four of these countries face serious domestic problems, which will be easier to solve in an Asian context than in isolation.

Unless solved, these problems could give rise to populism and nationalism, not only jeopardizing any attempts to work together but turning domestic problems into a genuine threat to further economic progress, and opening the door for political and social instability.

The Asian nation-states are, contrary to many analyses, not focused on foreign and security policy unless the outside world compels them to move such questions up the agenda. For each of them, the main problems and challenges are domestic ones. To synthesize this situation and perspective in a few words: Maintain social and political stability; the political leadership know better than anybody else that if the social structure starts to come apart the people can turn against the leadership.

Annex: Statistics[6]

A) Economics – Trade

Trade as share of GDP: China 38 per cent, India 41 per cent, Japan 31 per cent.

Export as share of GDP: China 19 per cent, India 19 per cent, Japan 16 per cent.

Balance of payments (2019 forecast): China +0.7 per cent, India –1.7 per cent, Japan + 3.6 per cent.

Comment/interpretation: Foreign trade contributes to growth in Japan and to a lesser extent in China, but it is a drag on growth in India.

Trading partners: *China*: Japan number 3 (deficit); India number 13 (surplus); half of China's trade is with Asia (small surplus). *India*: China number 1 (deficit); Japan number 15 (deficit). *Japan*: China number 1 (deficit); India not among the top 15. (ASEAN number 2.)

Top export destinations: *China*: United States, with Japan at number 3 and India about number 10. *India*: China and Hong Kong at number 3 and Japan about number 10. *Japan*: United States slightly above China.

Share of trade: *China's* trade with Japan is 2.6 per cent of its GDP and with India it is 0.6 per cent. *India's* trade with China is 4 per cent of its GDP and with Japan it is 0.8 per cent. *Japan's* trade with China is 6 per cent of its GDP and with India it is 0.30 per cent.

Dependence on the global value chain – import content of exports (share of gross exports, 2014): Japan 18.2 per cent, India 21 per cent, China 29.4 per cent. (United States 15.3 per cent.)

Overall observation on trade: Japan and India (Japan more so than India) are more dependent on trade with China than vice versa.

To the extent that China depends on the Northeast Asian supply chain, Korea and Taiwan may be more important than Japan. They are trading partners numbers 4 and 5, and both run a surplus with China, indicating that they sell intermediate goods to China compared to a Japanese deficit (2.2 per cent of total trade) and that trade is more skewed in favour of finished products. For example, the *Nikkei Asian Review* reported that exports of metal processing machinery jumped nearly 70 per cent as rising labour costs in China pushed companies to cut back on staff.[7]

Japan depends on finished products for its exports more than being in the supply chain. Japan seems still to be anchored in an economic structure where Japanese companies supply intermediate goods to other Japanese companies for final assembly.

An analysis of India's trade reveals that its alternatives to Asia are the Arab World, Africa (in particular East Africa) and Iran. As the *Arab News* reports, the Gulf is already India's principal source of energy and its major economic partner. There are about eight million Indians living in the region.[8]

India has emerged as Africa's fourth-largest trading partner behind China, the European Union and the United States, whilst Africa has emerged as India's sixth-largest trading partner behind the European Union, China, the UAE, the United States and ASEAN. It is to be noted that the volume of this was a meagre US$3 billion in 2001. Indian companies had already invested more than US$34 billion in the resource-rich continent by 2011, with further investments worth US$59.7 billion in the pipeline.[9]

India's trade relations with Iran are unbalanced as imports of oil are about seven times higher than exports (an annual figure of about US$3 billion, equal to 0.1 per cent of GDP), which mainly consist of rice and tea. But India is interested in maintaining economic and trade relations with Iran, seeing future possibilities. The country is also strategically positioned west of Pakistan.

B) Economics – Investment

Japan is the global leader in terms of its net international investment position, with China at number 3 and India as a net debtor country.

The 2018 forecast positioned Japan with a savings surplus of 3.8 per cent of GDP, China 0.6 per cent of GDP, and India with a savings deficit of 2.4 per cent of GDP.

Japan's ODI stocks in the ten largest economies in Asia, excluding China, reached US$259 billion in 2016, while Chinese ODI stocks in the same list of countries only reached US$58.3 billion. This excludes investments to Hong Kong, which, representing 60 per cent of China's total ODI flows, acts primarily as an intermediary of flows between China and the world.[10]

In 2017, Hong Kong was the largest investor in China. According to a report on the Santander Trade Portal, "Singapore, Taiwan, South Korea, Japan, the United States, the Netherlands, Germany, the United Kingdom and Denmark are other major investors. Investments were mainly oriented towards business services, manufacturing, trade, new technologies, real estate and financial intermediation."[11]

In terms of trade flows, Japan is the number 3 investing country in India. China is number 16.[12]

Comment/interpretation. Japan is by far the largest investor measured by amount and flow. China's stock and flow is somewhere between 5 and 10 per cent of the total FDI/ODI in Asia. India is only interesting as a recipient country, and is more dependent on other countries than on China or Japan.

Notes

1. This is an updated and amended version of an article first published on 13 February 2019 at YaleGlobal Online.
2. https://data.oecd.org/fdi/fdi-stocks.htm.
3. http://time.com/18147/climate-change-genghis-khan-mongolia/.
4. https://timesofindia.indiatimes.com/india/with-12-of-global-imports-india-tops-list-of-arms-buyers-report/articleshow/63276648.cms?from=mdr.
5. https://www.un.org/en/development/desa/population/publications/pdf/ageing/WPA2017_Highlights.pdf.
6. If not stated otherwise, the sources of data for the statistical annex are the IMF, the World Bank, UNCTAD, the Economist Economic and Financial Indicators and Baldwin and Lopez-Gonzalez, NBER working paper 18957, April 2013.
7. https://asia.nikkei.com/Economy/China-edges-out-US-as-Japan-s-top-export-market.
8. http://www.arabnews.com/node/1088901.
9. https://en.wikipedia.org/wiki/Africa%E2%80%93India_relations.

10. https://www.brinknews.com/asia/japan-outstrips-china-in-investment-in-asia/.
11. https://en.portal.santandertrade.com/establish-overseas/china/foreign-investment.
12. https://rbi.org.in/Scripts/AnnualReportPublications.aspx?Id=1221

9

Conclusions

There is little sign of a new social contract developing that would deliver a more equitable power structure and income/wealth distribution. On the contrary, power and wealth have become more concentrated. The elite seem to be tone deaf. There are too many parallels with the run-up to the French Revolution of 1789.

There is even less sign of a contract between humanity and nature, of mankind respecting nature and acknowledging the role of ecosystems as a fundamental factor underpinning the survival of the species. Humans still think that artificially engineered instruments are better than nature.

Despite the twelve fundamental challenges, the world is still ruled very much by mindsets forged during the industrial age and designed to deliver economic growth.

The future, up to 2035, based on what we know now about demography, technology and human behaviour, looks like this.

The world will become divided into regions, the three most important of which are Asia, the Western hemisphere, and Europe and its adjacent areas. The leading regional nation or nations will build their own technology—internet, 5G and such—energy grids and currency area, forcing other countries in the region into this strong economic, technological, cultural and political framework. This game is already visible for the United States and China. It will be difficult and expensive to do business outside the region, which points to a more compact supply chain.

Some elements of globalization will be maintained, but global institutions (the IMF, World Bank and WTO) and the global rule of law (for example, the United Nations Convention on the Law of the Sea) will wither away. Such a global model means that the world will stay entrenched in the current political and economic thinking without starting to shift gear and tackle the deep underlying challenges. Short-term economic profit will continue to control the actions of policymakers, as will the traditional power game.

The twelve fundamental challenges will be talked about but they will not be fundamentally addressed. Tepid national and international efforts will be insufficient to halt the threat they pose for civilization, or even less to set the course for a better world.

The World after 2035

Sometime around 2035, perhaps a little bit later, the challenges will reach the point where the disastrous consequences of having done too little, too late will be all too clear. Order and discipline inside nation-states and among nation-states will break down. Neither global rules nor regional agreements will be respected in this struggle for survival. Mankind will probably jump to technology as a last resort, despite the experience that clearly shows that whilst technology can help alleviate the problems, it is not a game changer that can save the world.

The question is whether biotechnology and digitalization can turn into ecosystems with the ability to repair themselves, or whether outside powers—data companies or governments or other institutions—will step in to control how social network can be used. Can we imitate the way ecosystems in nature promote such values in the biological realm, and transfer them to the socio-technological realm?[1]

As this is global, and cuts across any kind of cultural behaviour, it will inevitably determine whether digitalization turns out to deliver a "better" world or a sinister and egoistic world with people linking up in groups to confront other groups in a fight for resources, ultimately for survival, in a world of scarcities.

Conclusions

It is more likely that mankind will not be able to perform such a turnaround in attitudes, philosophical thinking and policies supported by a majority of the people. The core problem is that the solution requires reduced consumption in order to reduce pollution, global warming and the ruthless exploitation of resources. It is unlikely that populations in rich countries will agree to reduce their standards of living and transfer some of their consumption to the populations of poorer countries. It is equally unlikely that the populations of poorer countries will give up their ambitions to reach a standard of living comparable to those in the richer countries. The current flows of migration and refugees will be dwarfed by the number of people being driven from their homes by reduced resources, loss of farmland, rising sea levels and water shortages, to mention just a few.

In such a Darwinian world, steered by survival of the fittest, the following four scenarios seem the most likely:

1. Mankind rises to the challenge and tackles the problems of demographics, limited resources, climate change and water shortages, which will gradually lead to some form of global governance. There is however not much sign of this happening. It is a wonderful scenario, but it is the least likely one to occur.

   If this would be to happen, it could well originate from social networks and non-governmental organizations. An illustration of what might "save" the world is the fifteen-year-old Swedish schoolgirl Greta Thunberg, who started a school strike in August 2018 by sitting outside the Swedish parliament protesting against its inaction in combating climate change. Her protest has since spread to more than seventy countries and has gained global attention.[2]

2. A melt down of civilization as we know it. Unthinkable? If you believe so, recall the demise of the Roman Empire and the Chinese dynasties. It can happen because of fragility and complexity and a lack of understanding about our interactions with nature. Climate change and water shortage are crucial elements that manifest themselves mainly in Asia. Large coastal populations in China, India, Bangladesh, Indonesia and Vietnam are threatened should sea levels rise in accordance with the forecast.[3] India, Pakistan, Iran and parts of China are among the countries/regions that are

exposed to extremely high risks of water shortages. In time, the results of the total disregard for the long-term effects of chemicals and human tinkering may be even worse.

Combining the challenges of climate change, pollution, water shortages, poverty and lack of employment, South Asia seems to be most exposed, not the least because of its increasing population, which in some respects can stimulate the economy but risks being a drag on it, multiplying the problems should the political and economic environment turn sour.

3. A world ruled by semi-fascism and populism, albeit one still maintaining a façade of decency and able to maintain some kind of globalization. Samuel Huntington talked about a clash of civilizations.[4] He was correct in pointing out that culture, human behaviour and human attitudes play a more important role in politics than had been assumed. What is being seen now around the globe is a sweeping movement of antipathy vis-à-vis foreigners, even xenophobia. It will be difficult to maintain globalization if this attitude continues to gain ground.

    Several countries (for example Russia and Turkey) that looked to be on the course towards democracy have turned into illiberal democracies. In Europe the ideas that were behind fascism are rearing their ugly heads. In the United States the president is openly using vocabulary that would have been unthinkable just a few years ago. The main risk may come from what formerly were seen as the more or less impeccable democracies in Europe and the United States.

4. Dehumanization plus a delinking from nature making humanity depend on technology and taking our world into a strange state of anti-nature, which will not be able to last. This may be tempting for politicians, as some short-term benefits are to be seen.

    Such a scenario may come from powerful multinational companies, possible in an "unholy" alliance with governments and politicians.

The second half of the twentieth century held much promise for the future of mankind, even if as early as 1972 a report[5] had called attention to many of the problems dealt with in this book. There was a strong belief in the magic of new technology. The successful integration of China into the global economy gave rise to optimism that good governance was gaining ground. Institutionalized globalization and the UN system held the world together in what was generally perceived as catapulting the rule of law to the international level.

Over the course of about twenty years, this optimism and faith in the future have gradually yielded to pessimism about governance and the political system, and we now see something closer to angst about what the future has in store for mankind. The trend is more starkly visible in the developed (rich) nations than in the emerging markets and developing economies, which can be explained by the dramatic and positive decline in poverty in what used to be poorer nations, particularly in China.

It may be a task for future historians to explain why in such a short span of time that optimism and belief in the future, supported by a growing world economy, failed to produce an awareness of the challenges facing mankind or a willingness to address them.

My own guess is that the impediments to this have been caused by two basic human instincts. First, those who have power and wealth are not yet disposed to share it with those who have less; egoism is still too strong. Second, a number of studies demonstrate that in some cases people will show altruism, but watching today's world we see that the tribal instinct limits empathy and altruism to people like "us", while those who do not fall into this category increasingly fall as victims to xenophobia. Perhaps societies need an outside enemy in order to stick together, and they begin to fall apart if no common enemy exists, or alternatively they invent one, as seems to be the case with migrants and refugees.

The conclusion of this book is uncomfortable, and more so than most people would like to hear. Fortunately, nothing is carved in stone, and the human brain and mindsets have often been more flexible than expected. Time is certainly running out, but that is not the same as saying that humanity cannot reverse the negative trends discussed above. The first and most indispensable step is to focus on the threats and the unpleasant trends in the hope that this will enable mankind to reverse and set the course for a better future. There is still hope, but not if we are afraid of realizing that the future looks grim.

Notes

1. I am grateful to Arun Bala for having made this point.
2. https://www.theguardian.com/world/2019/mar/11/greta-thunberg-schoolgirl-climate-change-warrior-some-people-can-let-things-go-i-cant.
3. https://www.ncbi.nlm.nih.gov/pmc/articles/PMC4367969/.
4. Samuel P. Huntington, *The Clash of Civilizations and the Remaking of World Order* (New York: Simon and Schuster, 1996).
5. Donella H. Meadows, Dennis L. Meadows, Jørgen Randers, and William W. Behrens III, *The Limits to Growth* (Universe Books, 1972).

Epilogue: COVID-19[1]

COVID-19 has exacerbated and accelerated some trends:

- In geopolitics—the decline of US leadership, rising US-China tensions and the "demise" of multilateralism and rules-based order.
- On economic globalization—the trend towards regionalization[2] and economic nationalism.

More specifically, it has, for both the short and long term, added implications for:

- Economic recovery—whether it will be V-shaped, U-shaped or L-shaped.
- Societal structure
- Technology and data

The health aspects have attracted a lot of interest. The most important one may be: Are we prepared for another pandemic?

Geopolitics

American global leadership has been declining for some years. The US share of global GDP fell from 31.2 per cent in 2000 to 23.8 per cent in

2018.³ The same trend is visible for manufacturing, with the United States accounting for 16.6 per cent in 2018 compared to not many decades ago when it was the leading manufacturing country in the world.⁴ Debt is rising fast. It may still be the leading country for innovation and higher education, but the gap to challengers such as China is narrowing. There have been signs of an American strategic withdrawal for a decade or two in view of a mismatch between its capabilities and commitments.⁵ While the United States is unquestionably still the most powerful nation, its global outreach, capability and willingness to continue as global leader are not at the same level they were at the turn of the century. A cornerstone of President Trump's foreign and security policies has been to realign the costs and benefits of the US global role by cutting commitments. In some cases this has been manifested in the withdrawal of troops, as was the case in June 2020 with the announcement of a cut by a third of US troops in Germany. Such reductions, often made without any warning to allies, raises doubts about US credibility, and they may give rise to suspicions that US guarantees may be subordinated to presidential whims.⁶

For several years many observers have seen China as the next global leader.⁷ This conclusion may be too hasty. China's share of global GDP has risen from 7.2 per cent in 2000 to 15.8 per cent in 2018.⁸ This is remarkable, but it still leaves China far behind the United States. Even with the trends seen over the last decade, it will take quite a while before China is on par with the United States, especially if compared on the basis of GDP per capita. Recently, Chinese growth has slackened. For the first time ever, China has not set a growth target for the year. Enormous sums of money have been poured into R&D, focused on data systems and artificial intelligence, but it is still far from certain that these investments will deliver as hoped. China faces a demographic challenge, with a falling labour force and a growing share of elderly people, an overdependence on outside energy sources, and a service sector that is far less developed than that of the United States or those in Europe. On top of that, we do not know whether the Chinese leadership plans such a role, with the political and economic burdens it entails. The US experience illustrates that the position of being a global leader does not only bring benefits.

The trade war between the United States and China shows how the two powers have been testing each other. At the same time, it demonstrates how difficult it is to be a winner. The US dollar has been able to maintain its place as the only genuine global currency. The international monetary system is in reality a US dollar system, accounting for 90 per cent of all international transactions and with 60 per cent of all currency reserves being held in US dollars.[9] China is rolling out a digital currency, DCEP or e-RMB, which is the first of its kind to be backed by a country's central bank. It primarily has a domestic purpose—adding one more instrument to efforts to turn all money transactions in China into the digital sphere. It may also be seen as a Chinese attempt to undermine the role of the US dollar by offering this option to foreign countries that may be unhappy with the dominance of the dollar.[10]

When COVID-19 struck, both countries were found to be lacking in their attitude to the global picture. A global leader might have stepped in to shape an international, even a global, response to the challenge, possibly through the global institutions—the World Trade Organization, the International Monetary Fund and the World Bank. But neither of them did so.

They both struggled domestically when confronted with the crisis. The United States proved unable to cope with COVID-19. Despite the introduction of a health system under President Obama, it cannot be said to possess a genuine healthcare system covering the whole population. The fight between the president and state governors brought out in the open that the US Constitution is designed to weaken the federal government, making it difficult to implement nationwide policies. China's history gives ample evidence of the difficulties of keeping the nation together, which may explain why President Xi Jinping, since his election as president in 2012, has moved the country towards centralization. A more heavy-handed system and an even stronger role for the Communist Party of China (CPC) has emerged. Once the Chinese leadership decided to move on COVID-19, things went fast, and China was able to draw on nationwide resources to help Hubei province.

Some observers have used COVID-19 to debate whether democracy forms a better basis for combating an epidemic. It does not, however, appear to be the case. A study published at the end of May 2020—admittedly a little early—concluded that two things matter: the capacity of the state, and the degree of economic inequality. A strong state and governmental structures allow the authorities to act fast, and they serve as bulwarks against other shortcomings. Economic inequality normally means malnutrition, no money to pay for healthcare and the need to continue working, which facilitated the spread of the virus.[11]

COVID-19 makes the United States and China feel less secure and less confident. It is anybody's guess what that will mean for their stance in the global power game. If history tells us anything, it is that insecurity increases the likelihood of confrontation.[12] Political leaders may be tempted to look outside to score points in view of domestic criticism and discontent.

If such a development would be to take place, the fault line could be around Taiwan, which did very well in its fight against COVID-19. It has gained greater self-confidence and it may use this to get more leverage vis-à-vis China by counting on support from friends and looking for sympathy from abroad, particularly among Western democracies. This will provoke China, which would perceive such moves as a weakening of commitment to the One-China policy.[13]

Events in Hong Kong may also play a role in this game. China's plan to introduce a national security law[14] reveals a lower threshold for what it classifies as permissible in Hong Kong. The tension between elements of the Hong Kong population and China over the "one country, two systems" has been escalating in recent years. It has now reached a point where wide-ranging decisions will be taken. China regards it as an internal question, and it regards any interference as intolerable and provocative. The United States and some European countries, in particular Britain, have taken the view that China has gone too far and has violated the basic law. Politically, the United States does not feel the need to avoid any steps that could be seen by China as provocative, and it may search for an opportunity to look strong. At the end of May, the United States decided to declare that Hong Kong no longer enjoys a high degree of autonomy from China,[15] to revoke Hong Kong's preferential treatment as a separate customs and travel territory from the rest of China, to consider action against Chinese companies listed on US equities markets and to scrutinize the role of Chinese researchers entering the United States.[16] These decisions fitted the pattern of US behaviour, but may be ill-conceived. No country can ignore being at the receiving end of such actions. China has to respond.

The combination of a more assertive US, deviating from policies maintained over decades, dishing out this kind of behaviour from a weaker position, and with a more vulnerable China at the receiving end, looking to consolidate or even strengthen its role in Asia, is quite simply disquieting. There may be a genuine risk that a change in perceptions will push policymakers towards a confrontation. One of the things that carried the world through the Cold War was the ability of the United States and the Soviet Union to read each other's intentions. They were good at two things: at creating crises, but also at managing them. Misunderstandings were rare.[17] Both the United States and China seem determined *not* to work out such a common rule book.

Economic Globalization

Economic globalization is losing its primogeniture. The new model will be a mixture of globalization, regionalization and nation-state behaviour (economic nationalism).

Nation-states have stopped seeing the global system and its institutional framework as suitable for solving their problems. Very little has been heard from the United Nations. The International Monetary Fund (IMF) has assisted a large number of member states, which is commendable, but it has not undertaken any effort to map out an agreed global economic policy, mainly because member states have not asked it to do so.[18]

The United States and China no longer see globalization as benefitting both of them and they no longer trust each other. They each fear dependence on the other. From being "friendly" competitors inside the system, they now accuse each other of abusing the system. What may be even more important is that they, as the two dominating economic powers with forty per cent of global gross domestic product (GDP) between them, shirk their responsibility of running the system.

Regionalization has become fashionable because trust among adjacent nation-states pursuing analogous policies has crowded out global trust. Regional integration efforts such as the European Union and the Association of Southeast Asian Nations (ASEAN) may get new wind in their sails. While they failed to rise to the occasion to coordinate national measures in the first phase—the fight against the virus—they now may get a second chance when the battleground shifts to economics.

The costs of getting the economies back on track are enormous, and the prospect of doing the heavy lifting in common is much more attractive than trying it alone, for two reasons. The first is that the United States and the global institutions such as the IMF are largely absent from the game. The second is that if one country stimulates its economy while adjacent countries do not, it will run up unsustainable deficits on the balance of payments as imports go up. Some of the stimulus will benefit adjacent countries through trade. To avoid a game of musical chairs, where everybody tries to shift the burden of providing stimulus, coordinated efforts will be required.

Nation-states need to re-emerge as the guarantors of citizens' security and welfare—a role that was undermined during economic globalization. COVID-19 unmasked the non-economic costs of dependency on the global system, opening the door for autarchy, albeit watered down in most cases. The search for medical equipment, which in some cases turned into a scramble, served as an eye opener. The United States discovered that 30 per cent of generic drugs, accounting for the large majority of prescriptions, are imported from India, which in turn imports 68 per cent of the raw materials necessary to manufacture them from China.[19] In another sector, data systems, the world has for some time seen the United States on a major offensive to block the Chinese company Huawei from entering markets outside China.

The rising importance of regionalization poses a stronger challenge for China than for the United States. China was the big winner of economic globalization; it may be the big loser when regionalization and economic nationalism begin to have an effect. The global supply chain and the global value chain benefitted China, with its large, cheap and reasonably good labour force. But now with its falling labour force, wages are going to eat into its competitive advantage.

Outsourcing made countries dependent on one another. This was not fully digested, or perhaps it was and the price was deemed worth paying. In the future, nations will be more aware of how much goods and services they buy from outside, and how dependent they are on other countries. This turn around has hit China as the main global manufacturing hub. For some time, voices in the United States and Europe have been heard about the risks of relying on China and/or surrendering the technological edge to China by investing in foreign high-tech companies. In the future, the net will be cast much wider, and it will also focus on basic things like food and health.

The way out of this for China will be a greater emphasis on economic regionalization, in particular with the Belt and Road Initiative (BRI). COVID-19 has sowed or enhanced suspicion about China in the United States and Europe. It will push China to favour closer economic integration among Asian countries. It is possible that China will also use the BRI to boost manufacturing in Africa, for two reasons: to escape the rising Chinese labour costs, and as an alternative way to enter the European market.[20] It cannot, however, be taken for granted that such a strategy will succeed. Firstly, the Europeans will see it as it is—a way to circumvent the European barriers directed at China. Secondly, Africa may look promising but there is no certainty yet that it can live up to Chinese expectations. China also has its eyes on Latin America. The nexus may be that in the short term American and European markets will be indispensable, but in the long run what matters will be Africa and Latin America, plus possibly the Middle East and Iran.

The United States is less dependent on economic globalization than China. Its amount of trade as a share of GDP is 28 per cent compared to 38 per cent for China.[21] It is much less dependent on outside sources for basics such as food and energy. In the late 1990s, the then secretary of state Madeleine Albright often invoked the idea of the United States as the indispensable nation, conveying the calculation that all other countries needed the United States more than the United States needed them. As the largest economy in the world, and as the only nation with a genuine global capital market, this may still be true, although less so. But the fact is that China may scramble to seek outlets for its production abroad and sources for food and energy, while the United States enjoys the luxury of not having to put foreign markets at the top of its priorities.

It has recently become clearer that China not only envisages an economic network around Asia, Africa and Latin America through the BRI, but also a kind of technological, energy and possibly cultural co-operation. The thinking may be that such a network will encompass around 80 per cent of the global population, all the growing economies and around two thirds of global GDP. The potential mass of purchasing power is stunning. The Chinese offensive to sell technology to these countries may be part of this strategy, creating its own internet able to compete with the American one.

The US response has been curiously devoid of long-term strategic thinking. The purpose is apparently to stop China, trying to convince or even bully Western countries to follow suit, and to neglect alliances and partnerships outside the "Western" caucus. But the Western countries will not do well with regard to economic growth, and possibly also technology, because of the limited markets and the lack of funds in the wake of funding COVID-19 measures. It goes without saying that US policy during the Trump administration vis-à-vis its Western allies has not enhanced trust in the United States as a leader of the alliance. The United States looks increasingly to favour going it alone—and, in an analysis of global trends, without much promise of success in the long term.

It looks increasingly like a divided world.

Economic Outlook

With a few exceptions, countries have gone through the preceding decade trying to repair the damage done by the global financial crisis (2008–9). The hope was that gradually the economy would improve. COVID-19 torpedoed this prospect. The drive towards consolidation was stopped, and further COVID-19 stimulus measures have thrown an already unsteady economy into turmoil.

The economic outlook for the biggest economy in the world, the United States, is dismal. For the second quarter of 2020, the Federal Reserve System anticipates an economic contraction of up to 30 per cent, and an unemployment rate close to 25 per cent.[22] The Department of Labor has registered up to thirty million jobs lost. Figures like that have not been seen since the Great Depression of the 1930s.[23]

The European Central Bank has presented three scenarios that indicate that GDP for 2020 will plummet to between 5 and 12 per cent for the eurozone.[24]

China has lowered its economic growth target. For the first quarter of 2020, the economy contracted 6.8 per cent. The common view is that growth for 2020 may not be more than about 3 per cent.[25]

Japan is expected to go through a contraction of 5.2 per cent for 2020.[26]

Most analysts predict an economic upswing in 2021, but it cannot be taken for granted. Economic models tend to disregard social and behavioural repercussions. After COVID-19, people—consumers and businesses—may not go back to "as usual". The pandemic may have scared them, making it possible they will be reluctant to spend.

All countries have launched massive stimulus through budget deficits. This is understandable and in conformity with economic theory. If not, the economy would shrink even more than the figures given above. While it is good, indeed imperative, to do so in the short run, a number of problems arise for the future.

Governments need to consider how to rein in deficits, and in many cases how to repair the unavoidable damage done to national budgets. Where is the money to be found? From savings on other public policies such as transport, social security and education? From tax increases? From further borrowing? There are no easy solutions at hand. Most of those available point to tightening the economy, and running counter to the stimulus that has been launched.

Even before COVID-19, global total debt—incorporating governments, households, non-financial corporates and the financial sector—was following an alarming trend. From the third quarter of 2018 to the third quarter of 2019, it rose by approximately US$10 trillion, bringing it to US$253 trillion, which is 322 per cent of global GDP.[27] Remember, this increase took place when the economic global climate was benign. COVID-19 will propel global debt to an even higher level, while economic growth shifts downwards from 2.9 per cent in 2019 to a contraction of 3 per cent in 2020.[28] Higher debt needs to be financed by lower national incomes!

The Organization for Economic Co-operation and Development (OECD) calculates that the richest nations face a US$17 trillion government debt burden from COVID-19. For the thirty-seven member states, the average government financial liabilities will rise from 109 per cent of GDP to 137 per cent.[29]

In the United States, the Congressional Budget Office estimates that COVID-19 will hike the deficit on the federal budget from 4.9 per cent of GDP in 2019 to 17.9 per cent in 2020. An economic recovery will make the figure look somewhat better, but only reduce it to 9.8 per cent of GDP in 2021.[30] The total debt (government, households, non-financial corporates and the financial sector) in 2018 amounted to 265 per cent for the US GDP and 258 per cent for China.[31] The two biggest economies in the world were heavily indebted before the COVID-19 crisis, but have now escalated their borrowing. Such debt and deficits will cast a shadow over the economy in the years to come, narrowing the room of manoeuvre for economic policy.

The interest rate defines the sustainability of debt levels. Before the financial crisis, debt was on an upward curve. This trend accelerated during and after the financial crisis. Countries printed money to bail out the banking system and stimulate the economy. The dilemma was that rising debt would be incompatible with a stable economy. The answer policymakers came up with was a lax monetary policy delivering low interest rates. Debt levels that were not sustainable with interest at 5–6 per cent in 2000 became sustainable with interest at 0.6 per cent in 2019.[32] The following calculation shows how it works. In 2000 the US federal debt was US$5.6 trillion; with an interest rate of say 5.5 per cent, the net interest burden could roughly be calculated at US$308 billion. In 2019 the federal debt was US$22.7 trillion (about four times higher) and the net interest burden can be calculated to US$136 billion[33] (less than half).

The world has caught itself in a bind. Debt levels, after the explosive increase in the wake of COVID-19, will require interest rates close to zero. In reality, countries have committed themselves to maintaining monetary policies that history has shown cannot last more than a relatively short period. The interest rate is a price for borrowing and lending money. It plays an important role when banks calculate the ranking of investment projects. How can banks choose which investment projects to finance when the price for lending is close to zero?

The hitherto unanswered question is how countries will manage to return to a more balanced economy? How will it be possible to maintain a growth pattern, to roll back deficits and debt and to allow the interest rate to find a level in conformity with what can be termed "normal"—all at the same time? And what happens if they cannot do so? What will be done with the excess money? There is a considerable risk of a major financial crisis waiting in the wings.

Economists have often discussed whether the recovery after the COVID-19 crisis will be:

- V-shaped: fast and without much delay in getting back to the growth pattern of before the crisis;

- U-shaped: Some delay in the recovery, but returning within a reasonable period to the same growth pattern; or
- L-shaped: A fairly long stagnation or slow growth, without any certainty that the economy will return to what used to be normal growth.

The contraction in 2020 will be considerable. A fast recovery may be possible for some countries that had a robust economy before COVID-19. The picture is more worrying for already fragile economies. They may be further weakened. The most likely scenario for most countries is, unfortunately, a combination of U-shaped and L-shaped recovery.

Add to this the repercussion on prospects for the business sector—especially small and medium sized businesses—and the picture augurs an economic and social crisis. Many family businesses do not have the financial buffer to survive such a crisis. A large number of people stand to lose not only their income but also their identity, self-respect, self-worth and independence. Many of them will be in their fifties or sixties, with little opportunity of jumping into other sectors or acquiring new skills. Just think of tourism, which is one of the hardest-hit sectors.

Structural Changes

The business sector, and probably also the public sector, will perceive online work as a unique opportunity to save money. Facebook announced on 21 August 2020 that as many as half of its forty-five thousand employees will be working from home within ten years.[34]

Large office buildings are expensive, not least because they are normally located in high-rent business districts. The number of staff will be reduced, and many of those who are retained will be employed on short-term contracts. This will diminish the pension and welfare burdens for companies. The need for such benefits, however, does not go away, so the burden will be transferred to the public sector, which is already struggling to finance the existing programmes. Another question for public policy is what to do about a city infrastructure that has been built for commuters when less people actually commute?

The societal and cultural effect of more online work looks to be gigantic. Communication is a mixture of words, facial expression and body language. Personal experience tells us that there are certain things we only want to say to a person directly, face-to-face, in order to be able to see the reaction. Management cannot continue as usual. How will they be able to motivate staff? How can they determine who is qualified for promotion? How will they decide the wage structure? What happens to loyalty when staff never meet their colleagues or management and never come to a place that they associate with the company?

Outside the business sector, similar upheavals are visible. What does it mean for citizens' trust in the government and the public service if the personal contact, so vital for humans forming an opinion of others and their own situation, is increasingly replaced by digital contact?

Education is highly dependent on pedagogy, but how can teacher-student contact be maintained with the increase in digital contact at the expense of time spent in the classroom? When teaching in a classroom environment, the reaction and body language of the class provides a teacher with feedback as to how effective their message is being received by the students.

Societal life will see a reduction in human relations and an increase in digital contact. The next step may well be the introduction of artificial intelligence, gradually removing the human element in decision making. It is terrifying to ponder on the possible subjugation of decision making by a "machine" without the option to call on a human being as a last resort. It seems unavoidable that such a society will be steered by less solidarity, less empathy and less love for one's neighbour—a digital system cannot be programmed to incorporate these elements.

Technology and Data

Technology has developed to the point where the main theme of George Orwell's novel *1984* (a surveillance society) may be feasible, and COVID-19 has given this technology a raison d'être. It can alert people should they come too near to other human beings, in particular those suspected of being sick. This is attractive as an instrument in the fight against COVID-19. But it also means that the authorities have technology on hand to track citizens. It remains to be seen how far and how fast countries will move to introduce such technology, and whether it will be mandatory, introduced by incentives or voluntary.

As things stand, citizens of the large majority of countries need not fear surveillance motivated by political reasons, but no one knows the stance of those who will be in power a couple of decades from now. Perhaps they will be governed by a different set of values, making such surveillance perfectly legitimate. Perhaps not; we do not know. In another area, digital payments make it possible to monitor what each individual is buying and how citizens spend their money.

The big winners of this technology may not be governments, but rather the big data companies. They all give assurances that data about citizens and businesses are safe, but only they themselves know how they handle this data. The transfer of power in this regard—or, let us say, potential power—is of a size and impact not seen in human history since the feudal societies gave way to the industrial societies 250 years ago.

Governments, citizens and businesses may be left in the dark, not knowing exactly what kind of data the big companies have amassed, how it is stored and, most importantly, how it may be used by those who possess it. The possession of data in the future may come to be the most important power vector.

A crucial question is whether social media companies should be regarded as publishers or platforms? In other words, should they be obligated to host what people post, or can they perform edits? Currently, the United States protects social media from being responsible for the content posted by their users.[35] But that presupposes that they refrain from editing or removing posts unless they violate the law (for example, blasphemy). The companies have long maintained that they are platforms only, but the rising concern over fake news and abuse of the internet have forced them closer to editing. And if they engage in this, the rationale for their protection laid down in Section 230 of the 1996 Communications Decency Act becomes questionable, and the future of social networks as we know them today will be up in the air. Who is responsible for what we read on social networks, and who has the right to block or edit content? Recently, President Trump put his finger on the sore point of trying to limit the protection for social media. He did so after Twitter added a fact-checking tag to one of his tweets. It will take a while for the legislative system to chew on this. But the interesting point is that the role of social media has now been challenged.[36]

The data companies—or to be more exact, one of them, Facebook—have entered a completely new arena, which had hitherto been the sole privilege of governments: printing money. In the summer of 2019, Facebook announced it was planning a new global digital currency—Libra.[37] Governments did not hesitate long before expressing their dissatisfaction, saying that Libra would disrupt the financial system, facilitate money laundering and compete with fiat money like the US dollar.[38] There is little doubt that governments are scared. One comment about China's introduction of the e-RMB is that it was launched as a kind of counter attack on the Libra.[39]

COVID-19 provides an excuse for introducing new technology designed to register what citizens and businesses are doing. It ups the ante in the power game between the state and the data companies.

This also represents a treasure trove for criminals, terrorists and even foreign "unfriendly" countries. The hacking of private and public databases is a well-known phenomenon. Even if well protected, it has been seen over and over again that firewalls have been penetrated, opening the door for outsiders, whoever they may be.

In 2014, attackers got access to Yahoo databanks holding the personal data of up to a billion users.[40] In 2019, the American Medical Collection Agency system was attacked, and as a result the health data of about twenty-five million individuals was compromised.[41] In May 2020, EasyJet reported a highly sophisticated cyberattack that affected approximately nine million of its customers.[42]

Not only may COVID-19 accelerate a power shift of a colossal character, but is also demonstrates that new technology questions hitherto sacrosanct perceptions about privacy and security for citizens and businesses.

Health

This is not the first time in the last fifty years that we have seen how modern societies are vulnerable to a new virus. The progress in science and our knowledge have helped us to reduce but not to remove the danger of epidemics. The focus on COVID-19 has largely been on how to prevent it from spreading in communities, and the choice between a lock-down model or herd immunity. The strategy was to contain the virus, giving science time to find a vaccine. As far as can be seen, this strategy was successful, but we cannot be sure of the same good fortune when the next pandemic strikes. Vaccines are of course good, but mankind needs to be aware of the long-term risks of overdependence on medicine. Less biodiversity and less contact with nature makes our immune systems weaker, which undermines this first line of defence. And we may need it next time!

Four things look likely to happen.

The first one is a kind of screening to find and uncover where and how pandemics may start. In the case of COVID-19, there does not seem to be full agreement among experts, but the prevailing view is that it originated in bats and reached humans through an intermediary animal at a market for animals. Pangolins are often mentioned, but there is no certainty about this. Nor can it be ruled out that another route was taken by the virus to reach a vulnerable human being.

To uncover how COVID-19 originated and how it made the jump to humans is not only an academic question but is one vital for protecting us in the future. It is to be expected that a lot of money will be devoted to virology, immunology and similar disciplines.

The second step is to look into why there is no uniform pattern that can tell us whether a virus will spread, how contagious it will be, how many of the infected will die, and whether a second wave is likely. Policies need to be carefully calibrated to the potential danger, which is not always so easy to discern. Experience gained from earlier pandemics can be useful.

The SARS epidemic in 2003 hit twenty-three countries, with 8,422 cases globally, of which 7,665 were found in China, Taiwan and Hong Kong.[43] Even if it spread around the globe, it could not be rated as a full-scale pandemic.

In 2009 the world saw the appearance of H1N1, which, according to the US Centers for Disease Control and Prevention (CDC), claimed the lives of more than 150,000 people worldwide. Some 80 per cent of deaths were of people younger than sixty-five years of age.[44] This was almost the exact opposite of what happens in a "normal" flu epidemic—and indeed for COVID-19—with the large majority of deaths found among elderly people. The interpretation is that the H1N1 virus may have been around at an earlier date, possibly as another version, allowing the elderly people who would have been young at the time to build immunity, protecting them against the new version that occurred in 2009. This observation underlines the importance of the immune system, and represents a case where herd immunity apparently worked in the long run.

In 2012 the Middle East Respiratory Syndrome (MERS) arose in Saudi Arabia. It saw 2,521 cases, with 866 deaths reported, of which about 80 per cent occurred in Saudi Arabia.[45] Seen from outside the country, this epidemic was largely a local or regional phenomenon.

The third step will be for countries to build a comprehensive defence system around:

- Beefing up the horizon scan to enhance the ability to catch signs of a new virus.
- Contingency planning has worked well for many countries. However, COVID-19 may have disclosed some weak links and/or indicated where improvements might be useful.
- COVID-19 regrettably but understandably revealed that countries tend to protect themselves, which in some cases led to a scramble for medical equipment. It might be useful to fund an international stockpile of equipment. In the case of some outbreaks, MERS for example, only a few countries needed equipment, so there was no impetus for other countries to sit on the same equipment. An international effort will lower the cost of being prepared.
- Strengthen education and information about how an epidemic can be avoided or its impact lessened if it cannot be kept at bay or contained.
- A consultation and coordinating system among adjacent countries, preparing the ground for common policies if possible, instead of each country fending for itself.
- It has been depressing to watch the chaos in air traffic, with countries, airports and airlines acting with little or no coordination. Next time hopefully some kind of global coordination may ensure that a limited number of routes are kept open.

The onus will be on detecting future viruses, taking preventive measures as early as possible and calibrating the measures carefully.

Doing too much is as costly as doing too little, too late. It may be a tough balance to strike, but the advantages and savings in human lives and money of nipping a virus in the bud are enormous.

The fourth step will follow in one or two years' time, when it is known whether there was a second wave. Until that is behind us, it is difficult to judge which strategy proved to be the most successful one. More so, it will be crucial in determining strategies for in the event of future pandemics.

Some scientists link the severity of a second wave to the strength of immunity seen in the first wave. The line of thinking is that the populations of some countries will be less likely to become infected and to succumb to the virus than will be the case in other countries. But the reasons behind this will be difficult to pinpoint One study has compared Germany and Britain and concluded that the average German has more immunological "dark matter" than the average Briton. Scientists have likened this factor to dark matter because they know it is there—statistics have demonstrated it—but it is not known what it is. If it can be uncovered, and quickly, the knowledge can be used to protect people in the event of a second wave, as the defence can be targeted at those most likely to become infected, instead of targeting the whole population.[46]

The question of a second wave is one of the most intriguing things connected to COVID-19, and it will disclose one of the biggest gaps in our knowledge. As long as a second wave is still a risk, governments will tend to move cautiously, giving the economy lower priority. That also explains why a considerable amount of money devoted to future research will go towards this question.

Conclusion

Our societies face brutal, profound and opaque radical changes that can be compared to what happened in the aftermath of the industrial revolution. These changes would have taken place anyway, but COVID-19 has served as a catalyst. Perhaps history a hundred or two hundred years from now will conclude that these changes were more important than the epidemic itself.

Notes

1. Parts of this epilogue appeared on 12 May 2020 in *Berlingske Tidende* and on 31 May 2020 on the website of *The National Interest*.
2. For an assessment of the impact on ASEAN+3, see Jayant Menon, "Covid-19 and ASEAN+3: Impacts and Responses", *ISEAS Perspective* no. 2020/54, 28 May 2020.
3. https://data.worldbank.org/indicator/NY.GDP.MKTP.CD?locations=CN.
4. https://www.statista.com/chart/20858/top-10-countries-by-share-of-global-manufacturing-output/.
5. In 2011, Secretary of Defense Robert Gates warned European allies that they would have to pay more for their defence. https://www.reuters.com/article/us-usa-nato/gates-parting-shot-warns-nato-risks-irrelevance-idUSTRE7591JK20110610.
6. https://www.nytimes.com/2020/06/06/world/europe/germany-troop-withdrawal-america.html.
7. See, for example, Martin Jacques, *When China Rules the World* (Penguin Books, 2009).
8. https://data.worldbank.org/indicator/NY.GDP.MKTP.CD?locations=CN.
9. https://www.voanews.com/economy-business/chinas-digital-currency-takes-shape-will-it-challenge-dollar.
10. https://www.forbes.com/sites/rogerhuang/2020/05/25/china-will-use-its-digital-currency-to-compete-with-the-usd/#39055e9c31e8.
11. https://knowledge.wharton.upenn.edu/article/politics-pandemics-countries-respond-better-others/?utm_source=kw_newsletter&utm_medium=email&utm_campaign=2020-05-26.
12. There is a saying that two wounded royal tigers are more likely to fight each other than two fiery ones.
13. See an analysis of this by Wen-Ti Sung, "Taiwan's Covid-19 Diplomacy and WHO Participation: Losing the Battle but Winning the War?", *The Diplomat*, 2 June 2020, https://thediplomat.com/2020/06/taiwans-covid-19-diplomacy-and-who-participation-losing-the-battle-but-winning-the-war/.
14. https://www.ft.com/content/27f4c7d0-ef5c-409c-b7b1-6c8108b8d128.
15. https://edition.cnn.com/2020/05/27/politics/hong-kong-pompeo-certification/index.html.
16. https://www.scmp.com/news/world/united-states-canada/article/3086788/donald-trump-says-us-end-hong-kong-trade-privileges.
17. The Cuban missile crisis of 1962 is an exception.
18. The US decision to withdraw from the WHO and its sniping at the WTO are cases in point.

19. https://edition.cnn.com/2020/05/16/business-india/india-pharma-us-china-supply-china-intl-hnk/index.html.
20. https://www.scmp.com/news/china/diplomacy/article/3086968/china-finds-manufacturing-opportunities-low-wage-africa.
21. https://data.worldbank.org/indicator/NE.TRD.GNFS.ZS.
22. https://www.cnbc.com/2020/05/17/powell-says-jobless-rate-could-top-30percent-but-he-doesnt-see-another-depression.html.
23. https://www.cnbc.com/2020/04/30/us-weekly-jobless-claims.html.
24. https://www.ecb.europa.eu/pub/economic-bulletin/focus/2020/html/ecb.ebbox202003_01~767f86ae95.en.html.
25. https://www.ft.com/content/4c2c6642-04c4-4fc5-bf80-12591975c215.
26. https://country.eiu.com/japan.
27. https://www.iif.com/Portals/0/Files/content/Global%20Debt%20Monitor_January2020_vf.pdf.
28. https://www.imf.org/en/Publications/WEO/Issues/2020/04/14/weo-april-2020; https://www.imf.org/en/Publications/WEO/Issues/2020/01/20/weo-update-january2020.
29. https://www.ft.com/content/66164bbc-40c7-4d91-a318-a0b4dbe4193e.
30. https://www.crfb.org/blogs/cbo-updates-budget-projections-wake-covid-19 + https://www.cfr.org/backgrounder/national-debt-dilemma.
31. https://blogs.imf.org/2019/12/17/new-data-on-world-debt-a-dive-into-country-numbers/.
32. https://www.macrotrends.net/2016/10-year-treasury-bond-rate-yield-chart.
33. The figures used do not fully reflect the current debt burden of the federal government, as the overwhelming part of the debt goes back to times when the interest rate was much higher than 0.6 per cent, but they illustrate the future impact of the interest rate on the net interest burden.
34. https://www.washingtonpost.com/technology/2020/05/21/facebook-permanent-remote-work/; https://www.theverge.com/facebook/2020/5/21/21265699/facebook-remote-work-shift-workforce-permanent-covid-19-mark-zuckerberg-interview.
35. The European Union and many other countries do not have exactly the same legal provisions as the United States, but they go some way towards offering protection to the data companies. https://in.reuters.com/article/twitter-trump-executive-order-explainer/whats-in-the-law-protecting-internet-companies-and-can-trump-change-it-idINKBN235094?il=0.
36. https://www.wsj.com/articles/trump-to-sign-executive-order-targeting-social-media-11590681930?mod=djemalertNEWS.
37. https://libra.org/en-US/; https://www.ft.com/content/af6b1d48-90cc-11e9-aea1-2b1d33ac3271.

38. https://www.cnbc.com/2020/04/28/checkout-joins-facebook-backed-digital-currency-project-libra.html.
39. https://globalcoinresearch.com/2019/07/17/chinas-attitude-towards-libras-threat-towards-the-renminbi/.
40. https://www.bbc.com/news/world-us-canada-38324527.
41. https://healthitsecurity.com/news/46500-austin-pathology-patients-added-to-amca-data-breach-victims.
42. https://www.businesswire.com/news/home/20200519005737/en/EasyJet-Struck-Sophisticated-Cyber-Attack---9.
43. https://en.wikipedia.org/wiki/2002%E2%80%932004_SARS_outbreak.
44. https://www.cdc.gov/flu/pandemic-resources/2009-h1n1-pandemic.html.
45. https://en.wikipedia.org/wiki/Middle_East_respiratory_syndrome.
46. https://www.theguardian.com/world/2020/may/31/covid-19-expert-karl-friston-germany-may-have-more-immunological-dark-matter.

Index

A
ADB, 89
Affordable Care Act, 36
Afghanistan, 70, 140
Africa
  China and, 167
  colonialism and, 66–67
  dependency ratio, 108
  India and, 147, 152
  manufacturing in, 167
  refugees and, 44
  water stress in, 7
ageing populations, 10
Age of Anthropocene, 9–10
agriculture
  climate change and, 7
  dependence on chemicals of, 9
AI. *See* artificial intelligence (AI)
AIIB. *See* Asian Infrastructure Investment Bank (AIIB)
Aixtron, 77
Albright, Madeleine, 167
Alibaba
  control of the internet by, 55
  expansion abroad, 128
  growth of, 73
  market capitalization, 80–81
  personal data and, 79
Alphabet. *See* Google (Alphabet)
Amazon
  market capitalization, 80
  personal data and, 79
  submarine cables, 55
"America first" policy, 18, 89, 140
American Medical Collection Agency, cyberattack on, 174
ancestry groups in the United States, 66
Angola, oil supplies to China, 113
anti-intellectualism, 67
anti-trust legislation, 55
AOL, PRISM and, 81
Apple
  Ireland tax case, 17, 83
  market capitalization, 71, 80
  personal data and, 79
  PRISM and, 81
  suppliers, 23
artificial intelligence (AI)
  China's targets for, 111
  COVID-19 and, 172
  fake news and, 56–57

Internet of Things (IoT) and, 130
public services and, 47
as threat to mankind, 4
ASEAN. *See* Association of Southeast Asian Nations (ASEAN)
Asian Development Bank (ADB), 89
Asian financial crisis, 20, 22
Asian Flu, 6
Asian Infrastructure Investment Bank (AIIB), 89
Asimov, Isaac, 67
Association of Southeast Asian Nations (ASEAN)
    China and, 148
    globalization and, 105
    regionalization and, 125, 165
Australia
    Chinese investments in, 76
    labour share in, 24
Austria, non-native share of population, 42

B

Baidu
    control of the internet by, 55
    Cybersecurity Law and, 83
    personal data and, 79
Bala, Arun, 158
Bangladesh, labour force, 106
Bank of America, 23
Belt and Road Initiative (BRI)
    in Africa, 167
    competition for funding under, 138
    COVID-19 and, 167
    in India, 110
    infrastructure projects, 78, 88–89
    management of, 148
    motive for, 138–39
    share of ODI, 120–21
    State Grid of China and, 114
Beveridge Report (1942), 2
Big Brother, 47–48
biotechnology, 4–5, 111, 156
Black Death, 5
bonus pater familias, 48
Bramall, Edwin, 49

Brexit
    British Parliament and, 36
    Conservative Party and, 36
    DUP and, 36
    fake news and, 40
    manufacturing components and, 131
    the periphery and, 45
    "Polish plumber" slogan, 43
    "taking back control" slogan, 18, 124
    voter base for, 12, 35–36
BRI. *See* Belt and Road Initiative (BRI)
bribery, 75
British Royal Navy, 140
Bush, George H.W., 52
Bush, George W., 18, 52

C

California, feud with Donald Trump, 68
Callaghan, James, 39
Canada
    Chinese investments in, 77
    labour share in, 24
capitalism, 22–25, 58
censorship, 56–57, 61, 79, 83
Cheng Ho, 138
child sex abuse investigation, 49
China. *See also* Belt and Road Initiative (BRI)
    2035 projection for, 109, 114
    artificial intelligence (AI) targets by, 111
    ASEAN and, 148–49
    barriers to, 74–75
    corruption and, 75
    COVID-19 and, 163–64, 168
    data companies and, 55, 83–84
    demographics, 108, 162
    dependency ratio, 108
    economic model of, 72, 73, 75
    economy post World War II, 30
    fear of, 74, 76
    financial institutions in, 73
    foreign aid by, 89

Index

formation as nation-state, 66
globalization and, 69–70, 76, 88, 90, 165
global network of cooperation, 167–68
global supply chain, role in, 71
Hong Kong and, 153, 164
India and, 107, 148–50, 151–53
Japan and, 148–50, 151–53
labour force, 106
"Made in China 2025", 111
manufacturing in, 71, 106–7, 111, 130–31, 166
multinationals in, 72–73
overseas investments, 77–78, 107, 119–20
pharmaceutical supplies, 166
political stability, 73
power in Asia, 143
R&D spend by, 86, 110, 162
as rising power, 89
savings surplus of, 30
share of exports/imports to GDP, 137, 167
share of global GDP, 162
share of US treasury bonds, 98
skills development by, 73–74
sustainability and, 85–88, 111–12, 132–33
trade war with United States, 30, 113, 132, 138, 145, 162–63
China National Offshore Oil Corporation (CNOOC), 77
Chinese Investment Corporation (CIC), 72, 73
Chinese nationals abroad, 75–76
Churchill, Winston, 141
circular economy, 87
Citigroup, 23
citizens
  communication with, 3
  laws and, 50, 51
  migrants and, 42–43, 51
  politicians and, 48–49
  public authorities and, 27, 46–48, 50

public services and, 44–45, 46
welfare systems and, 38, 43
clash of civilizations, 158
Clausewitz, Carl von, 70
climate change
  2035 projection for, 157
  as catalyst for conflict, 7
  energy policies and, 133
  impact on ancient civilizations, 7–8, 141–42
  protests, 157
  refugees, 7
  as threat to mankind, 7–8
Clinton, Bill, 18, 51–52
CNOOC, 77
Cold War, 143, 164
Communications Decency Act 1996, 173
Communist Party of China (CPC)
  data companies and, 55, 83–84
  environmental policies of, 86
  increased role for, 163
complacency, 51–53
Comprehensive and Progressive Agreement for Trans-Pacific Partnership, 122
concentration of ownership, 23
Conservative Party, 36, 49
consolidating powers, 142–43
contributors to production, 10
copyright, 132
corporate social responsibility (CSR)
  in China, 75
  decline of, 48–49
  globalization and, 58–59
COVID-19
  artificial intelligence (AI) and, 172
  China and, 163–64
  data, personal and, 173
  debt and, 170
  democracy and, 163–64
  economic impact of, 162, 168–71
  education and, 172
  Facebook and, 171
  globalization and, 161, 166

global leadership during, 163
healthcare, 166
medical equipment, 166
origin, 175
privacy and, 174
second wave, 177
strategies, 174–76
structural change from, 171–72
technology and, 172–73
United States and, 163–64, 168–69
welfare and, 171
CPC. *See* Communist Party of China (CPC)
crude oil, 102, 113, 138–40, 146
CSR. *See* corporate social responsibility (CSR)
currencies
   DCEP/e-RMB, 163, 174
   Libra, 174
   renminbi, 101–2
   US dollar, 101–2, 133, 163, 174
   yen, 101
currency cooperation, 133
cyberattacks
   on American Medical Collection Agency, 174
   on EasyJet, 174
   on Maersk, 129
   on multinationals, 129
   on Yahoo, 174
cybercrime, 53–54
Cybersecurity Law, 83

D

Daddario, Emilio Q., 32n23
data, personal
   COVID-19 and, 173
   data companies and, 78–79
   European Union and, 82
   leaks of, 47, 81
   PRISM and, 81
   privatization and, 47
data companies
   control of the internet by, 55, 84
   COVID-19 and, 173

democracy and, 90
globalization and, 90
nationalism and, 84
personal data and, 78–79
United States and, 55, 81–82
DCEP, 163
debt, global, 168–69
decentralization, 57–58
declining powers, 142
decolonization, 2
deconcentration, 58
dehumanization, 46–48, 61, 158
democracy
   2035 projection for, 158
   attitudes towards, 60
   COVID-19 and, 163–64
   data companies and, 90
   globalization and, 90
   representativeness of, 36, 38
   Soviet collapse, impact on, 52–53
   Spinoza's prediction for, 35–36
   threat from social networking to, 53–57
Democratic Unionist Party (DUP), and Brexit, 36
demographics
   ageing populations, 10
   contributors to production, 10
   dependency ratio, 106, 108–9
   economic competitiveness and, 106
   elderly, 10, 24, 45–46, 108–9
   geopolitical clash and, 11
   interaction with technology and energy, 114
   resource shortages and, 10
Deng Xiaoping, reforms of 1979, 30, 106
Denmark
   as genuine nation-state, 65–66
   non-native share of population, 42
dependency ratio, 106, 108–9
destabilizing influences, 141
disease. *See also* COVID-19
   ancient civilizations and, 5–6
   H1N1, 175–76

Index

MERS, 176
nature and, 8–9
SARS, 6, 175
disinformation, 40
disruptive influences, 141
Doha Round, 122
Druzin, Bryan, 60
DUP, and Brexit, 36

E

EasyJet, cyberattack on, 174
economic divide, 1–2, 49
Edelman Trust Barometer, 13
EDMEs. *See* emerging markets and developing economies (EMDEs)
education
   COVID-19 and, 172
   manufacturing and, 11
   mismatch in skills from, 69
   social mobility and, 11–12
egoism, 2, 158
Eisenhower, Dwight D., expansion of social security, 2
elderly, 10, 24, 45–46, 108–9
elections, fake news and, 40
emerging markets and developing economies (EMDEs)
   China's role in, 75
   global economy and, 30
   globalization and, 28
   migration of jobs to, 29
employment
   impact of technology on, 25
   skills gap in, 25
energy, 112–14, 132, 162
environment. *See* nature; pollution; sustainability
Erdogan, Recep Tayyip, 18
e-RMB, 163, 174
European Central Bank, 168
European Commission
   Chinese overseas investments and, 77
   Circular Economy Action Plan, 87
   "Closing the Loop" action plan, 87
   EU-US privacy shield, 82
   tax and, 83
European Court of Justice, Apple tax case, 17, 83
European Union
   data companies and, 55, 82–83
   EU-regulation 2016/679, 82–83
   European Court of Justice, 17, 83
   globalization and, 105
   immigration and, 43
   personal data and, 82
   regionalization and, 165
   role in world politics, 30–31
   sustainability and, 87–88
eurozone, 168
extinction of animal species, 5

F

Facebook
   censorship by, 56
   control of the internet by, 55
   COVID-19 and, 171
   growth of, 73
   Libra, 174
   market capitalization, 80
   personal data and, 79
   PRISM and, 81
   submarine cables, 55, 80
fake news, 41, 56, 57, 173
FDI, 119, 120, 137
Federal Bureau of Investigation (FBI), 81
financial institutions
   in China, 73
   deconcentration of, 23
   in United States, 23, 100
Finland, 65–66
Fitch, 100
5G, 128–29
Five Star Movement, voter base of, 12
Foer, Franklin, 79
foreign aid, by China, 89
foreign direct investment (FDI), 119, 120, 137
fossil fuels, 112–13, 132, 137

fracking, 113
France
  arms sales to India, 146
  labour share in, 24
  non-native share of population, 42
freedom, personal, 35, 53, 61
freedom of expression on the internet, 83–84
French Revolution, 155

G
G7, 122
G20, 122
Gaddafi, Muammar, 75
gas, 112–13
Gates, Robert, 178n5
genetic engineering, 4, 111
Genghis Khan, 8
Germany
  COVID-19 and, 177
  empire, 138, 142
  formation as nation-state, 66
  labour share in, 24
  manufacturing value added as share of GDP, 29
  migrant workers in, 43
  non-native share of population, 42
  R&D spend by, 27, 110
  regionalization and, 123, 130–31
  technology transfers, blocking of, 77
  US troops in, 162
global economy, post World War II, 29–30
global financial crisis, 18, 20, 61, 101, 168
Global Innovation Index, 110
globalization
  2035 projection for, 155, 158
  attitudes to, 28–29
  business-community links and, 59
  China's role in, 69–70, 76, 88
  COVID-19 and, 162, 166
  development of, 105
  double standards in, 76
  EMDEs and, 28
  external diseconomies of, 20, 22, 69
  immigration and, 41, 69
  impact of pandemics on, 6
  impact of technology on, 20
  increased mobility of people under, 6
  institutionalization of, 89–90
  leader of, 85
  nation-states and, 69
  populism and, 158
  US and UK as defenders of, 18
  values/norms of, 56
global order. *See* world politics
global power structure, 88, 134
global supply chain
  barriers to, 6
  changes to, 117–21
  China and, 71, 123, 166
  multinationals and, 71
  United States and, 121
global trade, share by country, 118–19
global value chain, 118–19, 166
global warming, 21, 85, 86, 90, 157
Goldman Sachs, 23, 100
Google (Alphabet)
  control of the internet by, 55
  market capitalization, 80
  personal data and, 79
  PRISM and, 81
  submarine cables, 55, 80
Greater East Asia Co-Prosperity Sphere, 126
"Great Firewall of China", 128
Greece, attitudes to democracy in, 60
greenhouse gas emissions, 6–7, 87
Gulf War, 18, 70

H
H1N1, 175–76
hacking. *See* cyberattacks
Hayek, Friedrich, *The Road to Serfdom*, 38
health. *See also* disease

Index

effect of pollutants on, 9
healthcare
  COVID-19, 166
  decentralization of, 57–58
Heath, Edward, 49
Himalayas, 144
Hinkley Point C nuclear power station, 77
Hitler, Adolf, 62n2, 143
Hong Kong, 153, 161, 164, 175
Huawei, 110, 129, 138, 166
Hubei province, 163
human factor, 47, 112
human rights, push-back against, 75
Hungary, United States and, 52
Huntington, Samuel, 158

I

Iceland, 65–66
ICT. *See* information and communication technology (ICT)
IMF, 68, 122, 165, 166
immigration, 41–43
immunological "dark matter", 177
imperial preferences, 126
import substitution policies, 20
India
  arms purchases, 146
  China and, 114, 144, 147, 148–50, 151–53
  Chinese investments in, 107
  demographics, 109, 147
  dependency ratio, 108
  energy demands of, 132
  finances of, 107
  foreign policy of, 146–47
  formation as nation-state, 66
  Iran and, 146
  Japan and, 147–48
  labour force, 106
  manufacturing in, 114, 147–49
  multinationals, 72–73
  pharmaceutical supplies, 166
Indian Ocean, 140, 146

Indosat Ooredoo, 80
industrial change, 3, 12, 22–24
industrialization, 22
Industrie 4.0, 111
inequality
  capitalism and, 22–23
  education and, 60
  social mobility and, 59
information and communication technology (ICT)
  dehumanization of, 46–48
  economic growth and, 22
  impact of, 3
  nation-states and, 65
integration, social networking as barrier to, 42
intellectual property, 132
international institutions
  regionalization and, 125–26
  role in world politics, 17
  United States and, 18, 85
International Monetary Fund (IMF), 68, 122, 165, 166
internet
  access, 55
  control over, 54–55
  fake news and, 40
  technical standards, 54–55
  traffic algorithms, 79
  US power and, 127
  US presidential elections and, 55
  weaponized, 128
Internet of Things (IoT), 130
Internet Protocol Version, 129–30
intraregional trade, 117, 121
Iran, India and, 146
Iraq, oil supplies to China, 113
Iraq War, 18, 70, 97, 134
Israel, arms sales to India, 146
Italy
  attitudes to democracy in, 60
  formation as nation-state, 66
  labour share in, 24
  non-native share of population, 42

J
Japan
  China and, 148–50, 151–53
  COVID-19 and, 168
  demographics, 108, 147
  foreign policy of, 145–46, 147
  formation as nation-state, 66
  India and, 147–48
  labour share in, 24
  manufacturing value added as share of GDP, 29
  multinationals, 72–73
  power in Asia, 143
  R&D spend by, 110
  share of US treasury bonds, 98
  World War II, entry into, 143
Japanese Navy, 139
JP Morgan, 23
judiciary, independence of, 50

K
Kidston cattle station, 76
Korea
  China-Japan competition over, 146
  labour share in, 24
  multinationals, 72–73
  R&D spend by, 27
Korean War, 70
Kuka, 77

L
labour
  in China, 106, 152, 166–67
  ethnicity and, 25
  impact of capitalism on, 25
  industrial change and, 12
  in South Asia, 106–7
  training needs of, 26
Labour Party, membership of, 49
Latin America, 66, 167
Lattice Semiconductor Corporation, 77
Lau, Lawrence J., 135n5
law and the individual, 50
legal framework, changes in, 50–51
Lega Nord, voter base of, 12
Liberal Democrats, membership of, 49
Libra, 174
Libya, evacuation of Chinese nationals from, 75–76
life expectancy, 10
Li Keqiang, 20
LinkedIn, 79
Locke, John, 53
Louis XVI, 138

M
Macron, Emmanuel, protests against, 45
"Made in China 2025", 111
Maersk, cyberattack on, 129
malinformation, 40–41
manufacturing
  in Africa, 167
  changes in, 12, 23–24, 29, 69, 141
  in China, 71, 106–7, 111, 130–31, 166
  employment in, 25, 69
  in India, 114, 147–49
  pollution and, 21
  smart manufacturing, 130–31
  transit to Asia, 29–30
  in United Kingdom, 141
  in United States, 161–62
  valued added as share of GDP, 29
Massachusetts Institute of Technology, international students at, 12
May, Theresa, 36, 77
McCain, John, Affordable Care Act and, 36
media access, through social media, 53
medical equipment, COVID-19 and, 166
medicine
  dependence on, 8–9, 175
  ethics of, 4
MERS, 176
Mesthene, Emmanuel G., 32n21
Microsoft
  control of the internet by, 55
  market capitalization, 80

Index 189

personal data and, 79
PRISM and, 81
R&D by, 79
Middle East
  colonialism and, 66–67
  fossil fuels and, 113, 146
  Indian Ocean and, 146
  US policy and, 134
Middle East Respiratory Syndrome (MERS), 176
migration
  2035 projection for, 90
  climate change and, 7
  nation-states and, 65
misinformation, 40
mmWave, 129
Modi, Narendra, 147
Moody's, 100
Morgan Stanley, 23
multinationals
  concentration of business activities, 23, 72–73
  cyberattacks on, 129
  global supply chain and, 71
  power game between, 72, 73–78, 129
Myanmar, sanctions on, 18

N
Napoleon, 138, 142–43
National Development and Reform Commission of China, 77–78
National Energy Administration (China), 85–86
nationalism, 139
nation-states, 65–66, 69
NATO, 76, 97, 140
natural gas, 112–13
nature. *See also* pollution; sustainability
  2035 projection for, 158
  Age of Anthropocene, 9–10
  circular economy, 87
  counter-attack by, 6–7
  disease and, 8–9
  empires and, 141
  loss of diversity, 5
  man's interference in, 4, 8–10
Nature's index of scientific papers, 110–11
Netherlands, attitudes to democracy in, 60
Nexen, 77
9/11 attacks, 52
1984 (Orwell), 47–48, 172
Nobel Prize for Economics, 67
North Atlantic Treaty Organization (NATO), 76, 97, 140
Norway
  as genuine nation-state, 65–66
  non-native share of population, 42
nuclear energy, 77, 113

O
Obama, Barak, 122, 163
ODI, 119–21
OECD Convention on Combating Bribery of Foreign Public Officials in International Business Transactions, 75
oil, 102, 113, 138–40, 146
Oman, oil supplies to China, 113
Operation Midland, 49
opinion polls, on the United States, 95–96
Oracle, 23
Orwell, George, 47–48, 172
outgoing direct investment (ODI), 119–21
outsourcing, 12, 24, 166

P
Pacific Light Data Communication, 80
Pacific Ocean, 140
Pakistan
  Chinese foreign aid to, 89
  labour force, 106
PalTalk, PRISM and, 81
pandemics, 5–6, 161. *See also* COVID-19; H1N1

parallel societies, as result of immigration, 43
patents filed by country, 110
People's Liberation Army Navy, 139
periphery, the
   Brexit and, 45
   political elite and, 141
   privatization and, 44–46
pivot to Asia by United States, 144–45
political behaviour
   changing ruleset of, 18, 134
   decline of participation in, 49
   predictability of, 17
political elite
   change in style of, 18–19
   commercial activities of, 48
   decoupling from population, 11
   in empires, 141
   self-interest of, 39
political parties, 39, 49
politicians, trust in, 48
politics as a profession, 38–39
pollution
   2035 projection for, 157
   agricultural chemicals and, 9
   China and, 20, 133
   financial cost of, 20
   globalization impact on, 21
population. *See* demographics
populism
   education and, 11
   globalization and, 158
   regime change and, 139
poverty
   industrialization and, 22
   privatization and, 44–46
poverty trap, 29
power game, 69–88
PRISM, 81
privacy
   COVID-19 and, 174
   Orwell's Big Brother, 47–48
   personal data and, 55–56, 78–79
   privatization and, 47
   social networks and, 53

privatization, 44–46, 47
product cycle, 21, 87
Proliferation Security Initiative, 84
public services, 44–48
Putin, Vladimir, 18

R
R&D
   Apple and, 80
   China and, 86, 128, 162
   Microsoft and, 79
   spend by country, 27, 130
rating agencies, 100–101
RCEP, 88, 122, 148
Reagan, Ronald, 39
recycling, 21, 87
Regional Comprehensive Economic Partnership (RCEP), 88, 122, 148
regionalization
   change from globalization, 121–22, 155–56
   COVID-19 and, 165
   currency cooperation, 133
   "factories" of, 123, 130
   sovereignty and, 124
   spheres of interest, 126
   superpowers and, 126–27, 131
   values in, 123
renewable energy, 132–33
renminbi, 101–2
research and development. *See* R&D
resource shortages, 10
retirement age, 109
rights of the individual, 49–51
Rinehart, Gina, 76
rising powers, 142–43
rising sea levels, 7, 21, 157
Road to Serfdom, The (Hayek), 38
Roman Empire
   climate change impact on, 7, 141–42
   domestic forces impact on, 141
   mob rule impact on, 38
   patron-client relations of, 127
   plague impact on, 5
Roosevelt, Franklin D., new deal, 2

rule of law, as product of
  decolonization, 2
Russia. *See also* Soviet Union
  arms sales to India, 146
  Chinese foreign aid to, 89
  global order, place in, 18
  internet control and, 128
  oil supplies to China, 113
  power in Asia, 143
  R&D spend by, 27
  United States and, 52
  US 2016 presidential elections and, 40

S
SARS, 6, 175
Saudi Arabia
  MERS, 176
  oil supplies to China, 113
  United States and, 113
  US dollar and, 102
Schmidt, Eric, 128
scientific papers published by country, 110–11
Scottish independence, 66
Sea of Japan, 144
September 11 attacks, 52
Shanghai Cooperation, 123
Sina, Cybersecurity Law and, 83
Singtel, 80
Sino-centric power structure in Asia, 144, 148, 149
S. Kidman & Co., 76
skills gap, 25
Skype, PRISM and, 81
smart manufacturing, 131
social cohesiveness, 2
social contract, 2, 155
socialist parties, 38–39
social losers, 12, 25
social media. *See* social networks
social mobility, 11, 59
social networks
  2035 projection for, 156
  attitudes to democracy and, 61

  barrier to integration by, 42
  China and, 83–84
  Cybersecurity Law and, 83
  foreign policy through, 86
  immigration and, 42
  influence of, 67
  privacy and, 53
  protection for, 173
  responsibility of citizens for, 53, 61
  terrorists and, 53
  threat to free society by, 53–57
social security, expansion under Eisenhower, 2
soft power, of United States, 96–97, 101
South China Sea, 113, 140
sovereignty, 124–25
Soviet-Afghan War, 70
Soviet Union. *See also* Russia
  Cold War opposition to, 52
  collapse of, 18, 20
  economic model of, 19–20
  post-war years, 143
space programmes, 131
Spain
  attitudes to democracy in, 60
  Catalonian independence, 66
  non-native share of population, 42
  submarine cables, 80
Spanish Flu, 6
spheres of interest, 126
Spinoza, Baruch, Spinoza's prediction, 35–36
Standard & Poors, 100–101
State Grid of China, 114
stimulus measures, 168
Strait of Malacca, 113
sub-6, 129
Subpartners, 80
Suez Canal, 70
superpowers
  assets and citizens abroad, 75
  continental vs. maritime, 138
  grand strategies of, 137
  projection for 2030s, 115

regionalization and, 126–27, 131
spheres of interest, 126
Thucydides trap and, 70
trade routes and, 137, 138
transition of, 134
United States as, 18, 89, 96
Supreme Court, neutrality of, 50–51
surveillance, 172–73
sustainability
China and, 85–88, 111–12, 132–33
energy policies and, 133
European Union and, 87
globalization and, 90
policies for, 85–86
Sweden
arms sales to India, 146
attitudes to democracy in, 60
European Union and, 132
as genuine nation-state, 65–66
non-native share of population, 42
Volvo, 73, 132
Swedish parliament, 157
Syria, US withdrawal from, 140

T
Taiwan, 151, 164, 175
technical standards, 126–27, 129–30
technocracy, perspective of, 3
technology. *See also* artificial
 intelligence (AI); information and
 communication technology (ICT);
 R&D
2035 projection for, 156
adaptation to, 3, 26
COVID-19 and, 172–73
education and, 27
employment impact of, 24–25, 69
globalization and, 20
human relations and, 3, 27
interaction with demographics and
 energy, 114
patents filed by country, 110
skills demands of, 69
societal impact of, 27, 28, 69

speed of adoption of, 26–27
superpower competition over, 127
technology assessments, 28
technology transfers
blocking of, 77
China's policy for, 86, 132
telecommunications infrastructure, 80,
 128–29
Telstra, 80
Telxius, submarine cables, 80
Tencent
control of the internet by, 55
Cybersecurity Law and, 83
growth of, 73, 128
market capitalization, 80–81
personal data and, 79
terrorists
9/11 attacks, 52
social networks and, 53
Thaler, Richard, 67
Thirty Years War, 66, 70
threats to mankind, 5–9
Thucydides trap, 70
Thunberg, Greta, 157
Tibetan Plateau, 144
TPP, 30, 71, 88, 122
trade liberalization, 131
trade routes, superpowers and, 137
trade unions, socialist parties and, 38
Transatlantic Trade and Investment
 Partnership, 122
Trans-Pacific Partnership (TPP), 30,
 71, 88, 122
transparency, banking and, 58
treasury bonds, US, 98–99
tribal instinct, 158
Truman, Harry, 51–52
Trump, Donald
environmental policies of, 87
fake news and, 57
feud with California, 68
new class of politician, 18–19
social networking and, 39, 173
technology transfers, blocking of, 77

Trans-Pacific Partnership (TPP) and, 122
voter base of, 12
trust
  between citizens and politicians, 48, 49, 50, 60–61
  public services and, 46–48, 61
  social networks and, 61
Turkey
  migrant workers from, 43
  regionalization and, 134
  United States and, 52
Twitter, political impact of, 40

U

unemployment, in the United States, 168
unilateralism, United States and, 30
United Kingdom
  attitudes to democracy in, 60
  as defender of globalization, 18
  labour share in, 24
  manufacturing in, 141
  manufacturing value added as share of GDP, 29
  migrant workers in, 43
  Scottish independence, 66
  "take back control" policy, 18
  world politics, role in, 18, 29–30
United Nations
  decline in role of, 68, 165
  report on biodiversity, 5
United States
  alliances, 113–14, 132, 140, 144–45, 168
  "America first" policy, 18, 30, 89, 140
  ancestry groups in, 66
  arms sales to India, 146
  capital market, 99–100, 164, 167
  COVID-19 and, 161, 163–64, 168–69
  data companies and, 55, 81–82
  debt, 97–99, 121, 169–70
  defence spending, 140
  democracy and, 60
  demographics, 109–10
  dependency ratio, 108
  financial institutions in, 100
  global GDP share, 96
  globalization and, 18, 85, 97, 165
  Hong Kong and, 161
  image of, 52
  international institutions and, 18, 85
  internet dominance of, 127
  labour share in, 24
  manufacturing in, 161–62
  manufacturing value added as share of GDP, 29
  military, 96, 140, 162
  North American Free Trade Agreement and, 30
  opinion polls on, 95–96
  Paris Agreement and, 86
  pivot to Asia, 144–45
  power in Asia, 144
  presidential election 2016, 40, 55
  R&D spend by, 110
  role in world politics, 17–18, 29–30, 96, 97
  share of exports/imports to GDP, 137, 167
  share of global GDP, 161–62
  soft power, 96–97, 101
  technology transfers, blocking of, 77
  trade war with China, 30, 113, 132, 138, 145, 162–63
  Trans-Pacific Partnership (TPP) and, 30, 71
  treasury bonds, 98–99
  unemployment rate, 168
  waning power of, 89, 95–96, 134
Unocal, 77
UN Security Council, 17
US Constitution, 163
US dollar, 101–2, 133, 163, 174
US Navy, 88, 139
US presidential elections 2016, 40, 55
US treasury bonds, 98–99

V
value-added manufacturing, rank by country, 130
value-added trade, share by country, 118–19
Vietnam, Chinese investments in, 74
Vietnam War, 70
Volvo, 73, 132
Vo Nguyen Giap, 74

W
war
  global power structure and, 134
  global supply chain and, 71
  prospects for in Asia, 144–45
  results of, 70
  rising powers and, 142
  superpowers and, 137
water
  conflict over, 144
  shortages, 6–8, 157–58
welfare, 2, 38, 42–43, 171
welfare society, 2, 36–38
welfare tourism, 43
Wells Fargo, 23
Westphalian Peace (1648), 66
World Bank, 17, 68, 89
World Intellectual Property Organization (WIPO), 110
world politics
  EU role in, 30
  international institutions in, 17
  UK role in, 18, 29–30
  US role in, 17–18, 29–30
World Trade Organization (WTO), 17, 68, 122
World War I, 6, 142
World War II, 139–40, 142, 143
World Without Mind: The Existential Threat of Big Tech (Foer), 79
WTO, 17, 68, 122

X
xenophobia, 158
Xi Jinping, 72, 86, 88, 163

Y
Yahoo
  cyberattack on, 174
  PRISM and, 81
Yale School of Medicine, 4
Yeltsin, Boris, 18
yen, 101
YouTube, PRISM and, 81
Yugoslavia, 66

Z
ZTE, 110

About the Author

Joergen Oerstroem Moeller is a seasoned diplomat, having served as State-Secretary 1989–97 in the Royal Danish Foreign Ministry and from 1997 to 2005 as Denmark's Ambassador in Asia. Since 2005, he has been with the ISEAS – Yusof Ishak Institute, Singapore Management University and MFA Diplomatic Academy (Singapore), as well as the Copenhagen Business School and University of Copenhagen. He is a well-know futurist and author, having published *How Asia Can Shape the World* (2010), *The Global Economy in Transition* (2013) and *The Veil of Circumstance* (2016).

www.ingramcontent.com/pod-product-compliance
Lightning Source LLC
Chambersburg PA
CBHW070943230426
43666CB00011B/2542